Manufactured in the United States

Any resemblance to actual events or persons, living or dead, is entirely coincidental. This is in no form meant for harm nor do we promote harm. Personal perspective use only. Please do not copy/mimic any words or illustration from this book.

Cover Art by Cameron Wilson for Soulsimplicity Design and Publishing.

The old Black sharecropper, Pa-Ty McKie was born around 1881, at least according to Black African American oral history. Assuming the oral record is accurate, Pa-Ty was born about fifteen years after President Abraham Lincoln signed the Emancipation Proclamation. This document legally ended enslavement or involuntary servitude of all human beings (except for the "criminal"), within the confines of the "USA or any American territories."

Written and oral histories record that life for Pa-Ty McKie, as well as the other 4,000,000 newly "freed" Black Africans in South Carolina, Georgia, and throughout the southern United States was even more brutal after "emancipation," than during the days of "legal enslavement."

Pa-Ty strangely never discussed the experience with any degree of disdain, hatred, or revenge with his beloved grandson, Little George. He never discussed or complained about anything. The Black sharecropper, Pa-Ty McKie, rolled off his cotton and straw stuffed palette each morning, seven days a week, at five o'clock sharp.

His first task was to make a fire in the black iron potbellied stove in the front room of the rickety, old, wooden sharecropper shack that he, and his wife Nannie, and their 18 children called home.

Pa-Ty McKie went about his day making the best out of whatever, what he referred to as "Mama Nature," offered him each day to feed, clothe, and protect his family.

After years and years of unrelenting reaping and sowing, Pa-Ty McKie, who was born with an innate gift of financial practicality, at the time of his death had become the most industrious and "richest sharecropper" in the history of the Burke and Tillman plantations in Edgefield County, South Carolina.

Legend has it that he fathered 18 children, which was a powerful economic advantage under the southern sharecropper system. Not a single one of Pa-Ty's sons or daughters ever begged, stole, or starved.

It is the strongest desire of the author that the "secret" to financial independence, as taught by my granddaddy, the legendary, black 50% sharecropper, Pa-Ty McKie, to his beloved grandson, Little George, be read and properly interpreted to children throughout our community at the earliest possible age. "Every man deserves the dignity of financial independence." Within this short story lies the secret…

Dedication Page:
The Richest Black Man In Belair

This project is dedicated to the eternal memory of the, "Sharecropper Generation". The immediate descendants of those immortalized enslaved Africans scattered across the globe. Those heroes who made the conscious choice to stay attached to the land. To "work the land", until death, to keep their beloved families intact. To them I bow. Despite their harsh reality, somehow, they understood that the governing dynamic of human existence is the pursuit of happiness, meaning and purpose, which can only be experienced through the attachment to "family" and a "beloved community".

To my "adult children". Ericka, LG, and Moriah It is my greatest joy observing each of you practice mastery over your lives with such intelligence, confidence, and humility. It never ceases to amaze me how you have developed into such powerful individuals despite having been under the mentorship of such an imperfect dad.

My beloved grandchildren, MiMi, Cameron, Chase and Iyrie-Grace. You awarding me the unsolicited title of papa is my highest honor in life. I love each of you beyond measure or language. Humanity anxiously awaits the impact of your incredible intelligence.

A special dedication to Gwendolyn Cassandra Bowers Butler August 15th, 1986, we stood before God, family, friends, and state. We youthfully, and naïvely proclaimed that "only death shall part thee from me." 40 years later, amazingly, you still make me want to be "a better man." Without your unrelenting support, motivation, and occasional annoyances, this project would only exist in my imagination. Thanks so much for being you. This is truly a joint project. Wherever my literary projects take me, also, shall they take you. Again, thank you for being you.

TABLE OF CONTENTS

CHAPTER I
Sharecropping

At one o'clock in the afternoon, four million enslaved Black Africans received word that Abraham Lincoln had signed the Emancipation Proclamation. Finally, they were "free." In unison, they dropped their picks and shovels, patted the behinds of their beloved mules, and strutted off the sunbaked clay fields of the southern plantations and headed straight for town.

The administrator of the southern land bank had been warned that a gigantic wave of human blackness was approaching the town center with one purpose in mind: "That Lincoln fella had promised them 40 acres and a mule, and fifty dollars as reparation," for three hundred years of the most sadistic form of human enslavement ever recorded in human history.

Women, children, elderly, some as old as one hundred years, walked off the plantation that scorching hot and rainy summer day. A few wore tattered shoes, but many wore none. Most of the herculean Black males were bare chested.

They came and they came. The first march for black equality under law. Marching in the rain, under the stares of white disdain and horror, and hate. They marched to claim the Lincoln promise of 40 acres, a mule, fifty dollars, and freedom.

On this day, the cruel scheme of sharecropping was concocted. It didn't take long for the newly freed Black Africans to realize that Emancipation was a hoax. Few, if any, got the land or the fifty dollars.

Many of those who did were quickly tricked out of it, intimidated, or celebrated with too much enthusiasm. The land given, of course, was little more than dust fields. The mules were an overused surplus from the civil war. Bad land, near death mules, and no money was the reality of the emancipated Black African.

To add salt to their gaping wound, Abraham Lincoln ordered all northern troops out of the confederate territories. This olive branch to the confederacy left the stunned, unarmed Black population at the mercy of white southern, sadistic, projected hatred.

Lincoln left no firewall between the emancipated Black population and the vanquished white Confederacy. All the Confederacy had left after the loss of their blood-soaked utopia was shame, inner rage and four million Black men, women, and children to project it upon.

Sharecropping, as dehumanizing as it seems to us today, was the only survival option for most of the emancipated African population.

Pa-Ty McKie's father and mama swallowed their pride but never lowered their heads as they returned to the very same plantation emancipation liberated them from. They returned as sharecroppers.

Under the sharecropping contract, Black families were allowed to live, "free of charge," in the very slave huts they had abandoned in search of Abraham Lincoln's promise of freedom. They worked in the same fields. At harvest time, the profits from Black labor were split unevenly between the sharecropper and his new "master," the landowner.

CHAPTER 2
July I, 1881: High Noon

Pa-Ty McKie was born under the shade of a thicket of peach trees, on the edge of the old Tillman plantation, off highway 25 in Edgefield County, South Carolina in the tiny town of Trenton, South Carolina. If my great grandmama, Nannie Butler McKie, had fallen forward instead of backward, she would have landed stomach first upon the wooden plow that was being pulled by one of Mister Tillman's powerful mules.

Jabu, the huge Black overseer, realized after several minutes of yelling at Nannie to get up before Master Tillman rode through on his afternoon ride, that she was giving birth. Jabu nervously dragged Nannie under the shade of the peach orchard while yelling at the others to keep picking.

Jabu left Maggie, the oldest of the peach pickers behind with Nannie. He knew that he had to motivate the others to increase production to make up for the lost production caused by Nannie's collapse. He achieved it by the exercise of fear, intimidation, and kicks.

Jabu and two other pickers picked Nannie up out the dirt. They placed her atop filled peach crates stacked on the wagon. Pa-Ty McKie was born atop bouncing peach crates as the pickers picked their way down the peach orchard toward the tiny wooden McKie sharecropper shack. Pa-Ty was already hours old by the time they arrived at the shack.

I first recall meeting my granddaddy in 1958. I was about six or seven years old. I remember riding in the backseat of my uncle Ernest's shiny blue '58 Buick special, down the long red dirt road that snaked off highway 25.

I recalled the feeling of excitement as the wooden shack at the end of the red dirt road burst into view out of the dust. "Wake up Cecelia, wake up," I would yell. "Are we there yet?" she murmured as she stretched. Cecelia would always sleep all the way to granddaddy's house.

The old rickety wooden shack was supported high off the ground by stacks of red bricks glued together with sloppy white strips of cement. The four brick pillars were strategically placed at the four conners of the shack. I could see completely under the shack.

There were always three dogs and as many as eight or nine children playing under the shack each time we arrived. I have never seen all my cousins under one roof. The sounds of their joy continue to lease space in my memory to this day.

Granddaddy reportedly fathered and reared 18 children in that beautiful wooden shack. I later learned it was not uncommon for the men of Pa-Ty's day to father or breed large families, hopefully sons. The practice was driven by economic competition.

Under the new economic model of "share cropping," which replaced the previous economic model of legalized chattel slavery, the more children a sharecropper bred, the more peaches, peas, watermelon, and of course cotton could be picked.

Sons were highly favored. More sons meant higher productivity and increased profit for the sharecropper and the landlord. The children, or labor force, got no more out of the deal than they received during enslavement, which was nothing, according to my aunt Sallie Mae.

I got my first glimpse of granddaddy Pa-Ty through the dust kicked up by my uncle Ernest's '58 Buick Special, as we raced down the long and bouncy red dirt road toward the shack. Uncle Ernest was one of Pa-Ty's 13 powerful sons.

He was an excellent driver. We never felt scared, even at 90 miles per hour. Granddaddy Pa-Ty was known as one of the most industrious sharecroppers in Edgefield County South Carolina. He even owned a dairy cow and two mules. Most white sharecroppers did not even own a dairy cow or their own mule.

As we zoomed down the red dirt road, granddaddy Pa-Ty came slowly into view out the dust. There he was. He sat in an old, light brown wooden rocking chair. Most everything was made of wood during those slow hot days.

I could see the chair rocking slowly and serenely through the dust. It had to be late Sunday afternoon. Late Sunday afternoon, after church service at Old Macedonia, was the only time you would find Pa-Ty McKie in a state of rest.

He was a rather large man with skin that appeared to be stitched out of genuine, extremely worn black leather, a result of the efficient baking process of the Edgefield County sun.

Granddaddy's old brown wood rocker appeared to me as a golden throne. He sat in it with the posture of an African king, basking in the glory of his boundless empire.

Ever since that first glimpse of granddaddy Pa-Ty, I've felt that I carried the blood of royalty, if not extraterrestrial, within me. One of the first wisdoms of endless wealth granddaddy PaTy taught my oldest brother Little George, was to always stand with your shoulders back, chin up and always walk like you "belong to God."

"Keep ya enemies and the devil 'way from ya. Won't come within fifty miles of ya. Promise ya dat," Pa-Ty would always say.

I was practically an adult when I learned that granddaddy did not "own" the beautiful old wooden shack. Or the boundless land I roamed as a child, eating red watermelons that were sweet as cane syrup, and using huge golden peaches, baked to perfection by the Edge County sun, as rocks to destroy my imaginary enemies. I literally visited Wonderland every Sunday and sat at the feet of a wise African king. My granddaddy, Pa-Ty McKie.

Sharecropping was the natural manifestation of Abraham Lincoln's Emancipation Proclamation promise and reparation to the "freed" Black Africans previously enslaved in America." The white landowners desperately needed

Black labor. Blacks were in need, literally, of every substance required for survival.

After Lincoln seamlessly and cruelly pulled the Union troops back to the northern territories, the newly freed Black Africans were lost and practically helpless in a foreign land. They were left at the mercy of a hostile southern white population, driven by shame, inferiority and externalized self-hatred.

Was President Lincoln's actions moral or evil? The answer to the mystery is as deeply complex as the question of the actual cause or reason for the civil war itself.

History Scholars continue to debate if the Civil War was fought over "slavery," states' rights, or preservation of the so-called "union." The result of emancipation, however, is clear and undebatable. It was not the freedom anticipated by the Black African population.

To grant fifty dollars, 40 acres of poor dust land, and a near death surplus mule leftover from a long and bloody war, to a "people" who for two hundred years had been held in total bondage, victims of the most sadistic crimes against the concept of humanity ever recorded in 6,000 years of human history, in hindsight, appears to have been a cruel, insidious prank.

A people afforded only the realities of labor, physical, and psychological torture, forced reproduction, or breeding, daily male and female rape, followed by being thrown down into unmarked dark pit atop of a collection of hopefully already dead corpses.

Could such a people, after two hundred years of such a reality, be expected to possess the skill sets required to create an economically sustainable community?

Miraculously, when left alone they did. Despite the lack of fertile land, effective language, education, and equal protection under the law, they did. The unsolved mystery of how, is the stuff of legends.

This human achievement rivals the construction of the pyramids in the homeland. How could they have survived? Many even thrived. My granddaddy, PaTy McKie, was one of them. Trapped in "hell" with only his invisible God. Pa-Ty McKie not only survived, he prospered.

Mr. Burke, Pa-Ty's new landowner, provided him the dignity of the title of "sharecropper," rather than ex-slave. Under share cropping, the economic model in the south shifted from chattel slavery to debt slavery. The arrangement worked out "reasonably well" for both the parties, especially for the landowner.

The landowners regain the dignity of a highly productive, profitable, self- operating plantation system. The emancipated African sharecroppers were no longer "enslaved," and if industrious enough could unbelievably manage a small profit at harvest time. Most of course did not, but Pa-Ty McKie did.

The sharecropper arrangement, at least on the surface, was simple and at the level of theory, possessed a tinge of humanity. Under the arrangement, the landowner afforded the emancipated African a shack for himself and his family. He was also provided the required plows, picks, axes, shovels and mules, as well as endless acres of land to work.

With exceptional intelligence and discipline, he could possibly reap a small net profit at harvest. The main crops on the Burke Plantation were peaches, watermelon, asparagus and of course, cotton. The sharecropper and his sons, daughters, and wife worked the land sun up to sun down, usually six days a week, rain or shine, cold or hot.

CHAPTER 3
Thank God for Sundays

The landowner enthusiastically encouraged church attendance on Sunday. He would even loan the sharecroppers money to buy "church clothing." "Dressing up" for Sunday church services is one of the oldest practiced traditions in Black African American culture.

On Sunday, the Black sharecropper families looked as good, or better, and even more prosperous than the landowner and his family. "Dressing up" on Sunday mornings for church provided an "escape" and is a treasured tradition that is practiced to this very day within Black African American society.

The "dressing up" tradition in many African American communities is stronger today than during the enslavement and sharecropper era. Thank God for imagination.

The "dressing up" tradition became and continued to be extremely competitive, and even hostile within the African American society. The sharecropper families who could not compete were stigmatized, looked down upon by the better dressed sharecropper families. They soon became self- conscious.

Many stopped attending the more "affluent churches," and separated to start new churches for the "poor." The number of churches within the sharecropper culture exploded because of this inner community competition.

The landowners eagerly encouraged the competition. The landowners of course had ulterior motives for their encouragement. The landowners owned the dress shops. Sharecroppers paid high interest on the loans they were given to purchase their Sunday clothes. This scheme resulted in deeper debt control of the sharecropper by the landowner.

Landowners closely monitored the Sunday mornings services, or their Black appointee, usually the pastor. The sermons were frequently selected and approved by the landowners prior to delivery from the pulpit. The preachers were also selected or "called" to preach by the owner of the land.

The "called" Black preachers were usually the most articulate, charismatic, handsome, and usually lighter skinned among the men in the sharecropper community. They had to be willing to, or if not, intimidated or bribed into espousing "safe scriptures." Scriptures like, "Obey thy master...God never places more upon your back than thy can bare etc. and love thine enemy."

Perhaps the most effective of all religious indoctrination was the concept of a literal heaven after death. With heart breaking efficiency, the charismatic light skin Black pastor deeply indoctrinated innocent Black children prior to the developmental age of critical thinking with these psychologically devastating concepts.

The "called Black pastor" proved to be the most effective and ingenious instrument of social, psychological, and economic control over the Black sharecropper society and culture. "He" had near absolute and "Blessed assurance" that the emancipated African sharecropper would never seek and/ or even express the concept of humanity or liberty. He was usually rewarded heavenly for his assistance.

To judge the "Black pastor" however, is to demonstrate a severe lack of understanding and appreciation for context, as well as the complexities of hierarchies that exist among societies of all living species. Despite the tactic of intimidation and bribery, not all Black preachers were willing to participate in religious indoctrination of Black children and adults.

They managed to preach in a style and code that instilled hope, strength, wisdom, and authentic humanity. One of those Black preachers was my granddaddy, the Reverend Pa-Ty McKie.

Public expression of liberating theology could result in severe reprimand, economic sanction, or even death for the Black preacher during Pa-Ty McKie's day.

Only the most "radical," enlightened and skillful Black preacher would even attempt such a dangerous act. Pa-Ty McKie, our granddaddy was one of them.

The sharecropper economic model was designed to assure two outcomes. The first, being financial prosperity for the landowners. The second objective of course, was the perpetual debt enslavement of the emancipated African sharecropper society for all times.

Unlike the vast majority of the Black sharecroppers, who at harvest time found themselves in a vicious cycle of debt, Pa-Ty McKie managed to provide prosperity for the landowner, for himself and for his huge family.

At harvest time, the landowner received half and Pa-Ty received half. Pa-Ty McKie was what was known during those days as a 50% sharecropper. The status of being a 50% cropper was extremely rare among the Black and white sharecropper communities.

At harvest time Grandmamma and all the daughters got two new dresses each. Pa-Ty made all of the boys new leather shoes by hand. There were other perks that came along with a successful harvest as well, like store bought cookies and soda pop.

Unfortunately, that was not the reality for the vast majority of sharecroppers, black or white. Most sharecroppers never saw a profitable harvest. They died in debt leaving their families at the mercy of the profit driven landowner. The families were usually kicked off the land a week after the sharecropper's funeral. A new sharecropper family immediately and gladly replaced them.

A major contributor towards Pa-Ty McKie's financial success was Pa-Ty McKie's 50% contract.

You see, Pa- Ty McKie owned his own mule, Dalla. He owned two mules, as well as a milk cow. Equivalency in today's economy would be like owning two brand new Ford 150 and a super charged air-conditioned tractor.

A sharecropper who somehow managed to own his own mule received a 50% split at harvest time compared to the one third split received by sharecroppers who did not own a mule or other tools such as picks, plows, or wagons.

The second wisdom Pa-Ty drilled into his beloved grandson, Little George's head was "Don't never come in the field without ya own mule and tools." Pa-Ty would also say, "Man ain't got no tools, ain't much more than a boy with whiskers."

Pa-Ty would always end his wisdom statements with, "Ain't never gonna be no different." Pa-Ty McKie also managed to develop income streams separate from share cropping. This strategy significantly increased his profits.

Pa-Ty always told little George jokingly that a pie sweetened with profits is sweeter than one baked with wages. Pa-Ty McKie was a farmer, as well as a dirt floor sharecropper. Pa-Ty would say, share cropping profits the landowner, while farming profits the farmer.

Mr. Tilman nor Mr. Burke nor any of the other landowners in the Edgefield County plantation community cared anything about what the sharecropper did with the land immediately around the sharecropper shack. It could sometimes be as much as an acre or more.

Many of the sharecropper wives used the excess land to plant beautiful flowers. Pa-Ty saw an economic opportunity. At the end of each day, prior to putting up the mules for the night Pa-Ty would use every slice of daylight left, sometimes lantern light, to plow and plant melons, peas, tomatoes, greens, squash, and potatoes on every inch of the land surrounding his shack.

It was truly a sight to behold. On Saturday mornings, rain or shine, blistering hot or artic cold, Pa-Ty loaded the wagon and hitched it to his mules, the lead mule Dalla, and Mussel.

Pa-Ty's third wisdom he taught to his grandson little George was "Don't never git tied down wit' two lead mules. Be nothing but trouble."

Pa-Ty ran his household employing this philosophy as well. Dalla and Mussel pulled Pa-Ty and his wagon loaded down with vegetables all the way from Edgefield County, South Carolina to the farmers market on Gwinnett Street Extension in Augusta Ga. Dalla's leadership was never challenged by Mussel.

By high noon, all the vegetables were sold. The tin can under Pa-Ty's seat filled with coins. Only then would Pa-Ty, Dalla and Mussel head back to the shack. They usually made it back before dark. All three would get fed and watered.

Pa-Ty would flop into his old wooden rocker and wipe his brow with his dirty, worn, red and blue checkered handkerchief. He would tell a few ghost stories. Little George especially liked the one about the headless horseman who rode through the watermelon patch every night.

Pa-Ty most often fell asleep in his rocker with Little George and his cousins asleep at his feet. After only a few hours' sleep, Pa-Ty somehow managed to stand in the pulpit on Sunday mornings, dressed spicier than any landowner. He always arrived before any of the worshipers at the Old Macedonia Baptist church.

The old sharecropper maintained this schedule seven days a week for 75 years without interruption or gripe. I don't remember ever physically touching my granddaddy's beautiful black leathery skin. I grieve that truth to this day.

Unlike my brother Little George, currently the richest Black man in Belair. Little George spent lots of summers on the plantation with granddaddy and Grandmamma. He got to touch granddaddy's face often.

He loved nothing more than that precious little brown wooden shack that sat in the middle of the Burke plantation. Little George passed the story of the old and wise leathery skin sharecropper, my granddaddy, Pa-Ty McKie down to me.

For that I am forever grateful. It is my responsibility now, to pass these wisdoms down to my children, Ericka, Moriah and Leon (LG) George, and to my grandchildren.

With humility and grace, I humbly offer Pa-Ty McKie's secrets for obtaining boundless wealth, dignity, and liberty to you, my beloved readers. I promise each of you that as demonstrated by Little George, Pa-Ty McKie's favorite grandson, who became the richest Black man in Belair within a single generation, that if you apply these humble wisdoms effectively, your life will be filled with financial success beyond your wildest dreams.

By effectively applying these simple but profound and universal sharecropper insights to his life, with total commitment and discipline, Little George not only became the richest Black man in "Belair", but he may also be one of the richest in the nation.

His primary home is nestled in the middle of 23 acres of giant pines, fish ponds, and natural streams with wild vegetation as far as the eye can zoom. Families of deer and a multitude of other wildlife call his estate home. The estate has value in the millions of dollars.

At his leisure, he hunts, fishes, and boats. He golfs several days a week on the finest golf courses. He travels to any destination his heart desires with his devoted wife. Their marriage lasted 50 blissful years.

By following the wisdoms pass down from our granddaddy, Pa-Ty McKie, Little George, "the richest Black man in Belair," has carved out his own version of the" American dream," the garden of Eden.

Just like his beloved grandaddy the old sharecropper, Pa-Ty, Little George's family has always been the center of his universe. As of this date he and his devoted wife have gifted the world with two intelligent and humble, financially wise sons, and five grandchildren. As taught by grandaddy Pa-ty, he has constructed a financial firewall around them that no calamity can breach.

Little George, by activating these simple, but profound concepts, he achieved this amazing feat in a single generation.

Little George is the second oldest of five siblings. Interestingly, he is the only sibling who hasn't obtained a college degree. But, by far he is the "richest." He chose not to attend one day of college. Instead, Little George activated the power embedded within the insights passed down by our granddaddy, the old leather faced sharecropper, Pa-Ty McKie.

Being not one to boast or make a big deal of his amazing success, it was like pulling teeth with a screwdriver, which was the method Pa-Ty McKie used to remove painful, abscessed teeth from his own gums throughout the years, to persuade little George to share the secret wisdoms with me.

One day out of the blue he relented. "All that I am and all I hope to become, I owe to my granddaddy." Little George jokingly like to use President Abraham Lincolns' words when describing the influence our granddaddy teachings had upon him.

"Granddaddy taught me the sacred wisdom for achieving endless, boundless wealth, and happiness," Little George began. Granddaddy's method of teaching Little George included close observation and practical intervention. Pa-Ty never injected himself, or rarely did, unless Little George faced an obstacle, he could not navigate himself. His injections were direct, unambiguous.

Granddaddy did not engage in "back and forth discussions." The only time Pa Ty would assume an authoritative posture with Little George was when Little George hesitated about putting the first ten cents, he earned in his tin can and the second ten cents in the can for the preacher. This initially was a difficult concept for Little George to grasp.

Pa-Ty consistently and patiently observed for an opportunity to inject wisdom into his sometimes, hard-headed grandson. The first wisdom involved the chore of pilling wood for cooking and heating, the wood cutting chore.

Every morning, Pa-Ty would wake Little George up so that he could help his uncles gather the firewood from the wood pile.

The wood pile was about a hundred yards or so from the sharecropper shack. Enough wood had to be piled to last the entire day. Enough for cooking breakfast, dinner and supper as well as maintaining the fire constantly burning in the gathering room fireplace.

Uncle Bosie and Uncle Buddy complained and fussed to Pa-Ty because little George was not piling his share of the wood. They made fun of him. They called Little George names like 'city boy' or 'baby', even 'sissy'. Pa- Ty observed Little George as he struggled to meet his quota of wood each morning, but never intervened.

Finally, out of frustration, Little George appealed to granddaddy for relief. "Granddaddy I can't carry as much wood as Uncle Buddy and Uncle Bosie," Little George admitted. "They holler at me and are always making fun of me. They even called me a sissy. Can I do something else granddaddy?" Little George pleaded.

"Reckon not," Pa-Ty mumbled. "The wood gotta be cut and pile every day to stay alive."

Little George looked as if he wanted to sob. Granddaddy Pa Ty grinned slightly. Little George did not grin back. Pa-Ty did not share his grin with many folks. Pa-Ty leaned forward in his rickety, wooden, burgundy painted rocker, and extended his tough hands into the fireplace.

Little George thought Pa-Ty's hands were way too close to the logs that were burning blood red, but he didn't say anything. He just held his breath. Pa-Ty became quiet for a while. Little George was puzzled.

Pa-Ty again extended his hands closer to the red burning logs and flames. Suddenly Pa-Ty mumbled, "Get ya coat and come wit' me Lil' Bully." Lil' Bully is a name Pa-Ty often called Little
George. "Wrap up good now," Pa-Ty yelled.

Little George followed Pa-Ty deep into the woods behind the shack. "Keep up now!" Pa-Ty yelled. Little George said, "Okay," as he shivered.

It was bitter cold outside. Little George began to wonder if appealing to Pa-Ty for help with the firewood chore was a good idea. Pa-Ty now about 20 paces ahead of Little George suddenly stopped.

Little George noticed that Pa-Ty was looking down toward something on the ground. It appeared to be a small mound or hill. Little George ran to catch up. What Little George thought was a mound of dirt, was actually a large, dead, swollen, frozen dog.

The dog was covered with, what looked to Little George, to be large white ants. They appeared frozen too. Little "'George was shocked at the sight of the frozen dog. He recognized the dog. He had just seen the dog running through the woods a few days past.

"What happened to him?" Little George asked innocently and sadly.

"Ain't it clear boy?" Pa-Ty gruffed. "Little George," Pa-Ty asked softly, "what is the difference between that dog lying there frozen and your Grandmamma and your cousins back there sleeping at the house all warm and cozy like?"
Little George was puzzled and just stared down at the frozen dog. "I don't know," Little George said sheepishly.

"That firewood boy," Pa-Ty said. "If we don't pile that firewood every morning, your Grandmamma would freeze the death just like that dog. Would you want that Lil' Bully?" Pa-Ty asked.

"No sir," Little George answered, as he continued staring down at the frozen dog. Pa-Ty warmly wrapped his arm around Little George and pulled him close. Little George thought Pa-Ty's overalls smelled liked smoke from burning firewood. They trekked back through the woods in silence.

Day break greeted them at the shack. Little George would never complain about gathering wood again.

Little George thought, "Some things just has to get done," Pa-Ty McKie's favorite proverb. By the time Little George and Pa-Ty returned from the woods, Uncle Buddy and Bosie had gathered most of the wood for the day.

"Get over here you lazy whippersnapper and do your part!" Uncle Buddy yelled. Little George looked at Pa-Ty pitifully. "Go on boy, go on." Little George removed Pa-Ty's right arm from around his shoulders and dashed toward what was left of the wood pile. He was thinking that the cold morning pow-wow with granddaddy had not been for nothing.

"Get up boy, get up now!" Little George was awakened out of a blissful sleep. He slept atop the Croker sacks filled with straw and cotton on the floor in the back room of the old sharecropper shack. When he cleared the cobwebs from his eyes, he saw Pa-Ty standing over him, holding his black horse whip in his right hand.

PA-Ty always had the whip with him in the fields. It often came in handy when the mules decided that they could not pull the plow through the dirt any further. Pa-Ty could always change Dalla's mind with no more than two strikes from the whip across the behind.

Little George also had witnessed on multiple occasions Pa-Ty using that horse whip on Uncle Buddy and Uncle Bosie when it became clear they required extra motivation to get to the fields and behind the plow.

The skillful use of the horse whip was passed down to Pa-Ty from his daddy, who was taught the skilled use of the whip by his slave master, who frequently used it on him and the other enslaved Africans on the plantation, where he labored until his death and burial down the deep Black slave hole.

There are no historical records of Africans or Native Americans using the whip upon their children prior to contact with the "white man" of Europe. One of the behaviors of the European invaders that the native Americans found most strange, was the frequent beating of their women and children. Pa- Ty never, of course, used the whip upon his beloved Little George.

"Today is Saturday granddaddy," Little George mumbled. "I know that boy!" Pa-Ty barked. "I want you to ride with me to the farmers market. I wanna talk to you a little more about that firewood."

"Okay granddaddy," Little George mumbled as he used both of his closed fists to rub the sleep out of his eyes.

"I might even give you a dollar, Granddaddy Pa- Ty yelled back. Little George suddenly was wide awake.

CHAPTER 5

The Ride to Farmers Market

After extending the invitation to Little George to accompany him to the famers market in Augusta, Pa-Ty disappeared from the cold back room. Little George could hear the floors crack as Pa-Ty walked through the shack and out the front door. Pa-Ty had already loaded the wagon last night before going to bed.

After walking down the path to the shed, as he did every morning rain or shine, cold or baking hot, he forced open the ancient raggedy wooden door. He patted his lead mule, Dalla, on the behind and then Mussel. Pa-Ty said good morning to his beloved mules, with the kindness of a neighbor. "Good morning gal," Pa-Ty said with a slight smile.

Dalla made gruff sounds and bobbed her head up and down. Pa-Ty hung a large pail of breakfast around Dalla's neck, and while Dalla consumed her morning meal and water, Pa-Ty hitched the wagon and filled it to the brim with winter vegetables.

Little George was standing on the porch waiting for Pa-Ty to finish feeding and watering the mules. He was dressed in overalls, a purple corduroy shirt, Brogan work boots, and one of Pa-Ty's old straw hats, which was apparently way too big for his head. Pa- Ty laughed harder than Little George had ever seen him laugh before.

Pa-Ty yelled, "Go in the house and grab that breakfast your Grandmamma fixed for us and let's get going! We got a long ride ahead of us to Augusta." Little George quickly returned with the bucket of breakfast and handed it to Pa-Ty. After several unsuccessful attempts, Little George managed to climb onto the tall wagon.

Pa-Ty bellowed, "Grab that wool blanket from the back boy, and wrap it 'round you. It's gonna be cold for the first couple hours, at least until the sun break through the clouds." Pa-Ty gave Dalla a couple of gentle flaps with the straps and yelled, "Giddy up gal. Giddy up!" The first 30 minutes of the trip was in complete silence and darkness.

South Carolina plantations were colder and darker than any in the south. To Little George, Pa-Ty seemed to be communicating with powers unseen. Little George was just trying not to freeze to death.

There was no covering on the wagon. Dalla and Mussel didn't seem to notice anything except their next step. The mules did not require direction. Little George quietly thought, just as Pa-Ty promised, after about an hour and a half Mother Nature expressed kindness and mercy.

The powerful sun burst through the clouds. The marvel remained with him the entire day. Shortly after the sun's victory through the clouds, Little George was able to remove the heavy wool blanket from around his body. He was now able to fully appreciate the beautiful countryside of the Edgefield county plantation community.

Little George was particularly attracted to the huge white two- and three- story houses with large columns, and balconies extending from all the windows that they passed along the way.

"Those are some pretty houses granddaddy," Little George said. "Yep," Pa- Ty answered as he gave the mules a couple more swats with the strap. "How did they get so big granddaddy?" asked an excited Little George. Pa- Ty said, "Me, your uncles, and some of the other fellas around here built them that big."

Little George could not believe his ears. He asked incredulously, "Ya'll built those giant houses granddaddy?" "Yep, just like I just told ya.," Pa-Ty said. Little George gasped in awe, "Wow!"

Without being instructed, Dalla jerked left. The mules left the main road and headed down a very narrow and bumpy path through thick woods. "Watch your head through here," Pa-Ty warned little George. "These tree limbs and sticky bushes will rip your face off."

"Why are we coming through here granddaddy?" asked Little George.

"Short cut to the bridge to Augusta," Pa-Ty mumbled. About five miles down the narrow little path, Little George witnessed a sight that would be etched in his memory forever. Little George could not believe his own eyes. For the first time in his life, he finally came face to face with the back woods people.

Little George had heard scary stories about the back wood Black people all of his life. Until now, he thought the stories were just that, made up stories. Little George had never seen people that looked so poor. Their tiny unpainted wooden shacks were not much larger than the outhouse behind Pa-Ty McKie's old shack.

Little George noticed that two of the shacks didn't even have windows or doors. The tiny shacks offered little protection from the rain and cold. These were the Black families that fell through the safety net and cracks of the sharecropper system.

Most emancipated enslaved Black Africans never received the Lincoln promise of 40 acres, a mule, and fifty dollars. The sharecropper system literally protected them from brutal starvation. In order to meet the criteria of a sharecropper family, however, there had to be an able-bodied father with multiple able-bodied sons to perform the labor required to be a profitable investment for the landowner.

For the Black families whose fathers and brothers were killed in the war, imprisoned, or even lynched by night riders, they literally had nowhere to go, except deep into the back woods. In the back woods, they survived totally off what nature offered them. Their diet consisted of berries, nuts, and Carolina pecans.

Occasionally, a sick or injured bird dropped out of the sky. A rabbit, squirrel, or possum would sometimes stumble into their crude traps. All the men were ghostly skinny. The women and children were even skinnier. Little George had so many questions for granddaddy about the back wood Black people. Pa-Ty's answers would alter Little

George's entire view of the world and may be directly responsible for my big brother eventually becoming the "richest Black Man in "Belair. Pa- Ty's answers motivated Little George to build that financial fire wall around his family that nothing could ever get through.

Growing up in the "under privileged" areas of Augusta, Georgia, called the projects, Little George had witnessed what he thought was devastating poverty. He had never, however, observed the human conditions that awaited his sight, as Dalla bumped down the five-mile short cut path through the back woods of Edgefield County, South Carolina.

The first shack Pa-Ty and Little George passed was where the Ivey family lived. There were about twelve people on and about the front porch. Three severely malnourished mutt dogs were playing chase with three small, bony children under and around the tiny shack.

The shack had no windows. There was a large black cast-iron pot with a fire burning in it, just off the porch in the yard. Little George noticed that there was no smoke billowing from the chimney like there always was at Pa-Ty's house. He thought to himself that he had never visited granddaddy and Grand mamma's house when smoke was not flowing through the chimney and into the sky.

He knew that no smoke meant no heat and no food. Several grown men were standing around the black fire pot. Their hands were very close to the flames. Little George was speechless and very frightened, as the mules slowly trotted towards the shack. Suddenly, the silence was broken. The back woods people began waving and yelling. Little George was shocked that the skinny bodies had voices.

The men, women, and boney little children started yelling happily, and waving. "Ey Pa- Ty! Hey Pa-Ty!" The children and the dogs rushed towards Pa-Ty's wagon as if Santa Clause had arrived on Christmas morning.

"Hey Mr. Pa- Ty!," the children yelled as they jumped up and down. Pa-Ty climbed slowly and carefully down from the wagon and allowed each child to hug his legs until they had enough. Little George continued to stare in shock. Pa-Ty extended his right hand of fellowship to all the grown folks. Little George saw that several of the children did not have shoes though it was cold. In a few minutes, Little George would discover why everyone was making such a fuss over his granddaddy.

After freeing his legs from the grasps of the excited children, and the firm handshakes with the grown-ups, Pa-Ty walked to the back of the wagon. He lifted the plastic cover and pulled out a bucket filled with fresh laid eggs, three smoked hams from his smoke house and even a pail of fresh milk from the milk cow.

Mrs. Ivey wobbled weakly down the wooden steps and accepted the blessing. "Thanks Pa-Ty," she said softly. "Thank you so much." She also thanked Jesus.

"Thank you, ma'am," Pa-Ty answered as he looked towards the ground. Little George wondered why Pa- Ty said thank you to Mrs. Ivey. Pa-Ty then gave each of the children a peppermint stick. They acted as if they had tasted a piece of heaven.

Suddenly, a weak, hoarse voice came from the porch. "Thanks, you old coon!" Mr. Ivey yelled from his old rocker on the partially broken down porch. "Now git before I git my shot gun!" They both laughed.

"Okay I'm going sir!" Pa-Ty yelled back. The children chased Pa-Ty's wagon 100 or so yards, waving and screaming, "Bye Mr. Pa-Ty!" Pa-Ty, Little George, and the mules continued their journey to the farmer's market.

Little George witnessed scene after scene of the same unimaginable suffering. They passed desperate family after desperate family, as they bumped slowly through the back woods of Edgefield County. Pa-Ty stopped and gave each family they passed a sack filled with winter vegetables and· hams.

Little George finally broke his silence. "Granddaddy," he said, "are you Santa Clause or something like that?" Pa-Ty laughed loudly and said no. "We don't believe in nothing like that in these parts," Pa-Ty said, "every man help take care his neighbor if he can."

Little George then asked curiously, "Granddaddy, how much did they pay you for all that stuff?" "Nothing." Pa-Ty answered, as he encouraged Dalla to speed up her step with two flaps of the strap. Little George remained quiet and held on tighter as Dalla bumped and navigated the wagon, still filled to the brim with winter vegetables, through a rough patch of thick brush.

"Main road just ahead boy," Pa-Ty said. Little George was glad. "Once we get to the road, we won't have but about an hour left." Although relieved at the news, the wooden crate little George was using for a seat was getting' hard. Little George began to squirm around trying to find a more bearable sitting position.

Once reaching the main road, Highway 25 to Augusta, the crate seemed more bearable. There were other mules and wagons on the main road to the farmers market as well. It was now warm enough for Little George to unwrap the wool blanket from around his shoulders. He folded it and used it for a cushion.

Dalla and Mussel pulled, and pulled, and pulled, with no sign of the market in sight. Little George could not rid his mind of what he had witnessed in the back woods. He kept replaying the scene in his head.

"Shack after shack," he thought. Some with no windows, just thick plastic and paper. Some of the people didn't even have outhouses, like the outhouse at Pa Ty's house.

The vision of the conditions of those freezing and hungry people refused to leave Little George's mind. Equally, and perhaps more perplexing to Little George, was the fact that none of them offered to pay Pa-Ty a dime for all those vegetables. That thought made Little George slightly angry.

"What money boy?" Pa-Ty snapped.

"You know." Little George answered. "The money they owe you."

"Nobody owes me nothing boy." Pa-Ty grumbled. "Gittin' close now boy just about 10 miles to go." Little George managed to quiet his thoughts and curiosities for a while. The only sound for about five miles were the sounds of the mules, and the other 10 or so mules' hooves, landing against the road.

"Granddaddy?" Little George asked.

"Yeah boy..." Pa-Ty was getting' a little weary of Little George meddling.

"Granddaddy, what would happen to those people if you did not give that food to them?"

Pa-Ty said, "Remember that swollen dead dog in the woods behind the house that was covered with maggots?"

The vision of the dog and the odor creeped back into Little George's mind. He became a little sick and saddened. "Yeah," Little George answered. Little George was quiet the remaining three miles to Augusta, Georgia.

"Whoa, Dalla." Pa-Ty guided the mules through the throngs of other mules, wagons, and people, to his regular spot in the rear of the market. It was tight and crowded and smelly. "Let's go up front granddaddy, lotta spots up there."

"We can't go up there. This is my spot right here." "Why?" Little George pressed. "You want to make that dollar or not boy? If so, it's time to work. Be plenty of time for talking during the four-hour ride back to the house."

Within just a few minutes, storekeepers were lining up at Pa-Ty's wagon. In about 4 hours or so, Pa-Ty's wagon was entirely empty. Little George was very impressed.

"Reach back in there boy and grab that bucket of grub. Let's fatten ourselves before we head back," Pa-Ty said. "Grab that bale for the mules while you at it. They want get us back if they ain't full. Grab that bucket and fill it with water at that pump over there." Little George was ready for whatever was in Grandmamma Nannie's bucket.

He hastily uncovered the feast which included five fat biscuits, ten thick strips of smoked bacon from Pa-Ty's smoke house, a jar of golden-brown molasses, two hunks of cornbread, and a large pile of black-eyed peas from last night's supper.

Little George and Pa-Ty washed their lunch down with a jar of fresh butter milk. Little George really enjoyed having dinner alone with Pa- Ty for the first first time, just the two of them and the mules.

Pa-Ty shared what was left with Sharecropper Jennings and his two sons. Again, Little George was curious. He just couldn't figure out how Pa-Ty could afford to give so much food away or even why. He would not dare say a word in the presence of dinner guest though.

Besides, granddaddy promised that they would talk during the four-hour ride back to the plantation. Little George loved to hear Pa-Ty talk. He had never heard Pa-Ty speak more than three or four words at a time. He loved Pa- Ty's gruffy voice. Pa-Ty's voice seemed to make him feel warm and safe regardless of the weather.

Little George never worried about anything at all when he was around his granddaddy. Lots of people feared Pa-Ty's voice. Maybe because he carried that long whip all the time. Whenever Pa-Ty got agitated, everybody jumped. Little George would just laugh.

Everyone thought Little George was a little crazy for not being afraid when Pa-Ty became agitated. Pa-Ty never lifted the whip or even a hand to little George, not even to the day he died.

Pa-Ty seemed to have loved every soul he passed throughout his 90 years of plantation life. Seemed to understand everybody's condition. The ups and the downs were the two descriptions he used for whomever he passed.

Nothing ever rattled him. The only time he showed any feelings or emotions was when he talked about joining Little George's great grand pappy and mammy "down in the slave hole."

"One day soon, um going down in the slave hole," was Pa-Ty's favorite hymn. Little George never could find that song in the church hymnal.

CHAPTER 6
The Long Ride Back to The Burke Plantation
(Pa-Ty's Wisdom Passed Down to Little George)

By the time Pa-Ty fed his devoted mules and waited until all the water from the bucket was in their bellies, the other sharecroppers had already pulled out of the farmers market. "See ya on up the road!" Pa-Ty yelled to sharecropper Jennings as he and his sons trotted down the road. The one o'clock sun felt nice. Pa-Ty and Little George, as usual, were the last to leave the market for home.

"Giddy up gal." Little George noticed Pa-Ty reach into the inside of his overalls and pull out a dirty, wrinkled up, white handkerchief. The handkerchief was stuffed with dollars and quarters and some half dollar pieces. Little George had never seen so much money at one time in the same place. "What you so excited over boy?" Pa-Ty asked Little George.

"All that money yours, granddaddy?" Little George asked. "Reckon it is, it's in my hands ain't it?" Pa- Ty answered. "I don't steal or borrow from no man."

"Are you rich, granddaddy?" Little George was curious. "Reckon so. Any man who gotta full belly and don't owe no debt to no man is rich, I reckon. Some fellas are a little richer than other."

Little George could not stop staring at the dingy, old handkerchief stuffed with green dollars and silver coins. His eyes nor his mouth could close.

"Stop staring boy!" Pa- Ty barked. "Don't ever get excited about what's stuffed inside another man's handkerchief boy! Not now! Not never! You hear me boy?"

"Yes sir." Little George answered nervously.

Pa-Ty continued, "Another man handkerchief ain't got nothing to do with you. You got that boy?" Little George closed his mouth, looked away, and muttered softly, "Yes sir." He was quiet for the next three or four miles up the road. Suddenly, Pa-Ty reached into the dingy handkerchief again. He flipped Little George four quarters one at a time.

"Wahoo!" Little George yelled causing Dalla to stop in her tracks. Little George jumped so high he fell clean off the wagon onto the dusty road. For the first time ever, Little George saw Pa-Ty's mouth wide open and laughing with his entire body.

Little George looked around through the dirt and dust until he found all four of the quarters Pa-Ty had just flipped him. He then climbed embarrassingly back onto the wagon. Pa- Ty could hardly tap Dalla with the strap and force out a giddy up because he was laughing so hard.

Old Dalla and Mussel were laughing as well. "Giddy up!" Pa-Ty yelled as he continued to laugh. Dalla and Mussel began the slow bumpy pilgrimage back to Edgefield County. Another three miles up the road, Pa-Ty finally regained his composure.

"Feels pretty good to be rich um boy." Pa-Ty said to Little George.
"It ain't but a dollar granddaddy." Little George shot back arrogantly. Little George could immediately tell Pa-Ty was agitated by his arrogance, but it was too late. The silence returned for the next half mile or so.

"Let me see that dollar boy," Pa-Ty demanded. Little George hadn't realized that he had caused such a serious commotion. Little George slowly opened his left hand and returned the coins to Pa-Ty's hand. "I'm sorry granddaddy. I won't say that no more."

"I said let me see it boy, not give it to me to keep. The first thing you gotta do is start listenin'. A man want get nowhere in this world if he ain't got enough sense to listen. You understand that boy?" Pa-Ty's voice suddenly turned gentle.

"How much money you got in your pocket or anywhere in the world boy?" Pa-Ty gently asked.

      "All I got granddaddy are these four quarters."

Pa-Ty spoke again, "That's all you got in the whole entire world fella?
"Yes sir," Little George answered embarrassingly.

Pa-Ty barked, "No money under yo mattress or in a tin can that you keep hidden under the hay in ya barn?"

"No sir. I ain't got no tin can or no barn granddaddy."

Pa-Ty laughed so hard and loud. PA-Ty didn't stop laughing until the excruciating pain from his hernia made laughing impossible.

After the pain settled a bit, Pa-Ty grabbed Little George around his shoulders and squeezed him until Little George thought his eyeballs were going to pop right out of his head. Pa-Ty said jokingly, "Boy you ain't worth the salt in that corn bread we ate for supper last night."

Pa-Ty and Little George laughed really hard together. When the laughing finally stopped, Pa-Ty said, "Don't make no never mind, you rich today." Little George smiled and said, "I ain't rich granddaddy, you are."

Pa-Ty turned his solemn face toward Little George. Dalla obviously knew precisely where she was headed and needed no guidance. "Lil' Bully, ain't that a dollar in yo hand?"

"Yes sir." Little George answered.

"Is yo belly full? Yo wife and all of ya chullin bellies full?"

"Yes sir." Pa-Ty and Little George laughed hard again.

"Any man calling' on ya over a debt you owe him?"

"No sir."

"If that be the truth Lil' Bully, you one of the richest men in the world right ni. Remember Lil' Bully 'It ain't him who got most, but him who need the least,' the rich man boy.

 'Least that's what yo great grand pappy taught me before they threw 'em down the slave hole. Don't know who taught it to him...The preacher I reckon. Can you understand that Lil' Bully?"

"Uh huh, yessir." Little George said with lots of uncertainty. Little George and Pa-Ty enjoyed the country scenery in silence for a couple of miles.

Little George was the first to break the silence. "Granddaddy?"

"Yea boy?"

"Why you so rich and everybody else so poor?" Pa- Ty paused for a couple of seconds. "Little George, those people we saw on the way to Augusta, you know the ones' living in them giant house with the tall columns and balconies, you think they po'?"

Little George stuttered, "Well no sir."

Pa-Ty barked, "If you gotta question boy, make sho' it's a sensible one. Some folks rich. Some folks po'. Some folks are richer than others. Some folks are poorer than others. Po' folks always been here. Rich folks have always been here. Gonna always be that way I reckon. Giddy up gals! Giddy up!" Pa- Ty ordered the mules.

After a few more miles of silence, Little George blurted out "I don't ever wanna be poor granddaddy. I wanna be rich.

I'm gonna pray every night and ask God to never let me be poor. I always wanna be rich with lots a money, just like you granddaddy." Pa-Ty laughed again lightly. Little George continued his proclamation.

"I wanna be blessed just like God blessed those people that live in those big houses granddaddy." Pa-Ty laughed softly again and said, "Ain't no need bothering God 'bout it. He already give ya all he 'tend to." Pa-Ty patted Dalla.

"Giddy up ole gal." Little George was confused. Silence again returned to the wagon for a while. The only sounds were Dalla and Mussel's hooves hitting the dirt road.

The silence lasted about two miles or so. Pa-Ty broke the silence this time. "Little George?" "Yes granddaddy?"
"Your old granddaddy gittin' on in this old life. Was near 90 years old my last birthday."
"You are 90 years old granddaddy?" Little George asked in amazement.
"How old you think I am you little whippersnapper?" Pa-Ty asked.
"900," little George answered.

Pa-Ty laughed again with his whole body. "Got this here swelling' down my private part area. The right side. Sometimes it's big as a young watermelon. I cain't git about like I use to."

"Why don't you go to the doctor and get it fixed granddaddy?" Little George asked. "Do it hurt granddaddy?"

"Hurt most of the time. Been to the doctor up the road in Trenton. They say an operation might help."

"When you going to get your operation granddaddy?" Little George asked.

"Ain't never gonna git one." Pa-Ty answered matter of fact. "Doc say at my age ain't no need. Beside
I can't go in that hospital up there."

"Why granddaddy?" Little George asked.

Pa-Ty calmly answered, "'cause they won't let me."
"But, but, why?" Little George demanded.

Pa-Ty asked, "It's their hospital ain't it? Plus, I don't want
no doctor cutting' on me any way. Don't trust no man
around me with a knife sharper than mine. Besides, lots
of the white fellas they let in that place never be seen
again.

Except lying in the front of the church. Besides, they
can't keep me from my day down the slave hole, so ain't
no need a foolin' wit' it." Little George said, "You scarin'
me, granddaddy."

"Little George?" Pa-Ty asked.

"Yes granddaddy?" Little George replied.

"Don't want you to say another word all the way
home. Just want you to listen. Can you do that boy?"

"Yes sir, granddaddy, I can."

"Promise to keep your mouth tied shut all the way to the
house?" Granddaddy Pa-Ty insisted.

"Yes sir, granddaddy."

After about a mile of dirt road Pa-Ty finally spoke. "Lil'
Bully," he said, "you are a bright boy. You not like most
boys. You are curious. I feel it my duty to try and clear
up a few things in that hard head of yours' before I
join my pappy and mammy down in the slave hole. If I
don't some other crazy fella will. I wanna make sure you
hear it from your own granddaddy."

"Hear what granddaddy?" Little George asked curiously.

"The truth boy. I know you got questions about

the things you see round here. The po, the rich. The colored, the white. I know you curious boy. It ain't fair to bring a boy up into this peculiar world and not explain things to him. Boy might grow up thinking something wrong with him and his kind.

If you try and figure it out on your own or listen to the wrong fellas and go about trying to change things the wrong way, you gonna end up down the slave hole with me and your great pappy and mammy before your time. May happen anyway."

Little George could not hold back his curiosity any longer. "What's the slave hole granddaddy?" Little George finally got the courage to ask.

Pa-Ty said, "We will get to that at the right time. I want you to get the whole story, so you won't go running' off like a chicken with its head cut off."

"What story granddaddy?"

"The story of the condition of our people in America. Not just our condition, but the condition of mankind and our relationship with God. You say you want to be rich right?"

"Yes sir." Little George answered.

Pa-Ty continued. "Then listen carefully and follow all that I am about to tell you and you will be one of the richest men of your generation. Will you listen to me Little George, without interruption?"

"I will granddaddy. I will!" Little George promised.

Pa-Ty took a few minutes to gather his thoughts, and his feelings. "Before I start I wanna clear up one thing in that big head of yours."

Little George was listening. "What is that granddaddy?"

Pa-Ty said, "Always play by the rule no matter where you find yourself, no matter what game you playing. No matter what advantage the other fella got. Every game got a set of rules."

Little George said, "I know that granddaddy."

Pa-Ty asked little George kindly, "Do you know that there is a rule that governs all games?"

"All games granddaddy?" Little George asked curiously.

"Yes, and it's important that you understand that." Pa-Ty said.

"What is that rule granddaddy? Is it the golden rule you once told me about? The one that says, 'the fella got the gold makes the rule.'"

Pa-Ty smiled and said, "That's the second golden. The first golden rule is even more important."

"What is it granddaddy? What is it!" Little George could barely hold in his excitement.

"Hold your britches boy. It's simple. Just treat every fella you meet along the road to becoming a big shot the same way you want the fella to treat you. No matter what you been told about him. If you stick to this rule, you'll be just fine in the end Little George."

Little George responded. "Granddaddy, that's easy."

"Wait until you hear the story," Pa-Ty said. "We came from a place called Africa."
Little George could not hold his excitement any longer. "I know that granddaddy," he blurted out. I learned about that country in geography and history classes at my school."

"Africa ain't no country boy!" Pa-Ty snapped. "Thought you supposed to be quiet anyway?" Pa-Ty was clearly agitated that Little George had interrupted him. "How long you been 'tending that school of yours?

Little George sheepishly said, "Seven years granddaddy."

Pa-Ty snapped again. "And you don't know the difference between a country and a continent yet?"

"No sir." Little George softly answered.

"You been paying attention at school boy? Can't learned nothing if you don't pay attention boy!" Pa-Ty barked.
"I pay attention granddaddy."

"Why you ain't learned the difference between a continent and a country yet then? Your great grand pappy taught me that back down in the woods before I was six years old." Little George asked,

"Why were you taught down in the woods granddaddy?" "Can't keep a man a slave if ya don't keep him dumb boy," Pa-Ty said. "Your great grand pappy would have been slaughtered worse than a pig at the slaughterhouse if he was caught teaching us bout Africa or anything else.

Little George had witnessed pigs and cows being slaughtered on many occasions. He imagined his great granddaddy being treated that way. He became queasy. "Why granddaddy," he asked, "why would great granddaddy be slaughtered for teaching you about Africa?"

"Simple boy. Like I said before. Ya let a man get some sense in his head, hard to keep him a slave. Almost impossible. Guess that's what is happening to y'all at that schoolhouse. They keeping' y'all dumber than a mule."

Pa-Ty laughed. He noticed Little George seemed sad. "What's the matter boy?" he asked.

"Nothing" Little George answered sheepishly. "I know you, Lil' Bully. I hit a nerve I guessed." Little George said, "Sometimes my teacher writes our lesson on the black board granddaddy."

"What difference does that make boy? Ya still gotta pay attention to learn boy." Pa-Ty answered.

Little George suddenly blurted out, "I can't see the board granddaddy."

"You can't see the board? You got two eyes ain't ya?"

"You know I got two eyes granddaddy." Little George laughed again.

Pa-Ty joked a little more, "Do you keep em closed while you at the schoolhouse?"

Little George laughed and tried to get serious. "I can't see things from far away granddaddy, for real."

"You trying to say you need eyeglasses boy?" Pa- Ty asked. That's what the teacher say," Little George said.
"Why ain't you told your daddy you need glasses before now?"
Little George said quietly, "My teacher sent a letter home last year."

Now Pa-Ty was curious. "Why ain't you got your glasses then?"

"Daddy said that if the teacher think that I need glasses, she can buy them herself."

Pa-Ty said, "I'll tend to that. Right now though, you gotta learn how things got in this mess. If you hear it from the wrong fella, you might go around hating' folk and blaming' folk.

Hatred the worse disease there is and it don't change a drop a history, the present, or the future. You got that boy?"

 Little George softly answered, "Yes sir."

Pa-Ty shook his head from side to side and said, "Humans beings a mess boy. At least most of 'em. Now, will you be quiet the rest of the way? When I get through, if you have any questions left in that head of yours, I'll answer them tonight after chores. If that brain in that big head work at all you won't have any."

 Pa-Ty and Little George both laughed. "If you listen and obey, by the end of the story you will know everything you ever will need to become the richest man of your generation. You wanna be rich don't you boy?"

 "Yeesss sir, granddaddy!" Little George yelled.

 Pa-Ty, Little George, and the mules slowly bumped along the road toward the Burke plantation. They were quiet for about 3 miles or so before Pa-Ty started talking again.

 "According to stories told by your great grand and your great-great grand pappy, life back home in Africa was good, always warm and sunny. Giant rivers, oceans, and beautiful wild animals roamed the land freely.

To get supper, all a boy had to do was climb up a tree or shake it real hard and supper would fall down on his head. My pappy, your great grand pappy, told me that Africa is really the Garden of Eden they speak of in the Bible."

"The garden of Eden, we come from the garden granddaddy?" Little George couldn't help but to ask.

"That's right boy," Pa-Ty said. Little George could hardly believe his own ears. Pa-Ty said, "Hold your britches, there is a heap more to the story."

Pa-Ty said, "Africa ain't the real name. Used to be called other names before it was called Africa." Little George was really curious. "What was it called granddaddy?" he asked.

"The original name, according to your great grand pappy, was Alkebulan." Little George tried to pronounce the name but soon gave up. "What does that name mean granddaddy?" Pa-Ty said, "My pappy told me that it means 'the mother of mankind' or as I said earlier, it also means the Garden of Eden."

"We really came from the Garden of Eden granddaddy?" Little George asked with excitement.

Pa-Ty said, "Reckon so." Silence returned. Only the sound of the mule's hooves hitting the dirt road could be heard.

The question bouncing around in Little George's head was why we left the garden in the first place to come here. Especially those poor Black people back in the woods standing around the fire barrel.

"Granddaddy?" "Yea boy."

"Why did we leave? Why did we leave the garden?" Little George finally asked.

"Leave where?" Pa-Ty snapped again. "The garden?"

"Well according to your great grandpappy, some fellas got a little restless. Started wandering around like fools. Some human beings ain't never satisfied even in the Garden of Eden. Some left seeking more food to eat.

Some were chased out by giant creatures. There were lots of giant and wild creatures running around the garden back then. Bigger fellas were around bullying some other fellas. Didn't have no shot guns back then. Some fellas just born curious. They wander the earth all their days."

"But how did we get way over here?" Little George asked. "According to your great grand pappy," Pa- Ty went on, "the earliest humans walked."

"All the way from Africa?" Little George exclaimed. "Reckon so." Pa-Ty answered. "Later, many others came by ship."

"All the way from Africa!" Little George asked again.

Pa-Ty responded. "Yep! According to your great grand pappy, my pappy, we wandered out the garden. We wandered the earth for thousands of years. Ended up all over the planet. A bunch a' fellas stayed put though. Didn't feel no need to wander I reckon."

"They're still back home in the garden granddaddy?"
Little George asked.

"Yep. What's left any way," Pa-Ty said. "Things gotta little
rough over the years. Some of your kin back home doing
real good. Some doing real poorly, nearly starving to
death."

Little George wanted to know, "Can I go to Africa
granddaddy?"

"When you become a rich man, you can go anywhere on
this earth," Pa-Ty said. "Reckon before long, a man rich
enough will be able to leave poor folks on this planet. Be
able to purchase a ticket to a better planet. Maybe all the
way the heaven." Pa-Ty and George laughed.

"I'm going granddaddy, I'm going to Africa!" Little
George proclaimed. There was another mile of silence.
Little George then asked, "Is that the end of the story
granddaddy?"

"Afraid not boy," Pa-Ty answered. "As I said, we wandered
all over the earth for tens of thousands of years before we
ended up here. A bunch of your cousins wandered way up
north into the mountains, the frozen ice country.

Pappy, say they got trapped up in those cold mountains for
over ten thousand years. A period of time the
schoolteachers called the ice age. Solid cold for ten
thousand straight years, according to your great grand
pappy.

So much ice and cold up in those mountains and caves,
the good Lawd didn't even check on them when he came
to Earth once."

"Wow!" Little George said with amazement. "Ten
thousand years in the freezing cold?" Little George
asked softly.

"Colder than that." Pa-Ty snapped.

"This story makes me sad granddaddy. What did our
cousins eat?"

"Not much. Anything they could find I reckon. They made the choice to wander up into those mountains.""What's the name of the mountains granddaddy? Can I go see them too when I get rich?" Little George asked.

"Didn't have no name back den. The book fellas today call them the Caucasus mountains. As I said before, a rich man can go where he want to, any time he want to. Don't know why you wanna go up there though. The good Lawd didn't even go there."

The silence between them this time was longer than the others. Finally, Little George asked, "What happen to them granddaddy? Our cousins up there in those cold caves? Are there any left?"

Little George thought quietly that after 10,000 years with no sun, no vegetables no watermelon or peaches, there couldn't be.

"Strange thing happen," Pa-Ty said. "According to your great grandpappy, one morning out of the blue, the sun rose over the mountains. God showed mercy I reckon. The ice melted a bit, not a lot. It warmed up enough for your cousins, who after ten thousand years, imprisoned in the ice, were able to climb down those mountains. They were some happy fellas. They had never felt the sun on their skin before that morning."

"Did they come back home to Africa?" asked Little George.

"Yes," Pa-Ty said, "but not the way they left. Didn't have no memory of Africa, nothing else for that matter. All they knew was the cold and the ice. Africa didn't remember them either. 10,000 years is a long-time." Pa-Ty reminded Little George.

"Was their a big celebration granddaddy?"

"Nope." answered Pa-Ty. "Why?" Little
George asked.

Pa-Ty paused for a moment as he patted the mules gently
with the straps. "Things were different. Your cousins had
somehow survived a mean and brutal ten-thousand-year
winter. Those frozen mountains had shown no mercy, no
kindness.

When a man ain't shown no mercy from the moment he is
born, he don't have no mercy to show the earth. All we
got to give the earth boy is what the earth gives us. A
mean, vicious, and brutal life turns' a fella mean, vicious,
and brutal. It ain't never gonna be no different.

Enough hunger turns him to something even he don't
recognize. Ain't no man no different. If a man get hungry
enough, their ain't nothing he want to eat or slaughter. He'll
even slaughter, and eat other men. He can't ever get
enough doesn't matter how much you feed him. Don't ever
let a man in your sight get that hungry boy. You hear me
boy?"

"Yes sir." Little George responded. "Granddaddy why
should I worry about other people?"

Pa-Ty said, "Because if you don't, you nor your family can
sleep peacefully at night. Always give the fella something
to eat if you can, without starving your own family."

"Granddaddy is that why you gave those poor families
living back in the woods all of our food and didn't get no
pay for it?"

"I didn't give it all to them," Pa-Ty said, "and I did get paid.
Never give a fella your last. Be happy to share your extra
though. I guess the best part of gittin' wealthy is being
able to share with your fella man," Pa-Ty said.

"Strange how it just make a man feel good to do good. Ain't
no man no different. You will see once you get your fortune.
Now let's get back to your cousins. Where was I?" Pa-Ty
asked.

Little George said, "You were telling me the part about how the cold and hunger and being treated unkindly all your days will turn a fella vicious and brutal."

Pa-Ty laughed and said, "You have been listening to me Lil' Bully." Pa-Ty continued.

"When your cousins stormed down those mountains after 10,000 years on the edge of starvation, merciless cold, constant fear, and danger around every corner, they had no concept of mercy or love. They even forgot God.

Survival was their only natural instinct. The environment was so mean, even deprived them of sunlight. No sunshine, no vegetables. They didn't even have fire to cook the frozen animals they seldom ran across.

The harsh, cold, dark climate caused their skin color to pale. Their eyes became multi colored. Red, blue, green, every color you can imagine. Their hair turned stringy and grew long down their backs to keep their neck from freezing solid.

Hair eventually covered their entire bodies which enable them to survive the cold climate. Ten thousand years of relentless starvation and seeing your family members die every day before your eyes, drive any fella near completely mad. Do the same thing to you and me. You understand that boy?" Pa-Ty barked.

All Little George could say was "Wow!"

"When they finally returned to the garden, they were unrecognizable. Some Africans thought they were devils. Some Africans thought they were Gods. There was no memory of who they really were. When they returned to the garden they went on a feeding frenzy.

The world they discovered was no match for their tenacity, brutality, hunger, unbelievable savagery. They ate everything in sight. Some story tellers say they even ate people."

Little George was horrified by the thought and vision of eating another human being.

Little George covered both of his ears with his hands and closed his eyes as tight as he could.

Pa-Ty yelled, "Snap out it boy! Climb down off of your high horse. You think you better than your cousins out of the mountains, don't you boy? "Little George didn't say a word. He kept his hands over his ears and his eyes shut tight.

"Well, you ain't!" Pa-Ty insisted. "You get hungry enough, you will eat these two mules and me for dessert. Ain't no man no different. Ain't never gonna be no different. A rich man gotta be practical boy," Pa-Ty said.

"You still wanna be rich boy?" Pa-Ty abruptly broke the silence that had fallen over the wagon again. "You ready to move past that nasty bit of human history and focus on your goal, richness and wealth?"

"Yes, granddaddy!" Little George said excitedly. Pa-Ty smiled, "Giddy up Dalla, let's take Little George back to our little slice of paradise."

CHAPTER 7
Pa-Ty's Wisdoms

"First boy, you gotta understand the difference between richness and wealth." Pa-Ty began. Next, we will talk about that little problem between you and yo' Uncle Buddy and Bosie 'bout collecting firewood for the house. Be quite ni. Got just a short ride left. You do wanna be rich, don't ya?"

Pa-Ty paused a moment before continuing with his insight. "Wealth is easy to obtain among men boy. Most men ain't worth the salt in dey bread though. Wealth is everywhere.... There's just so many people too lazy to work. Some are too sick to work.

Some men simply don't know how to do nothin'. Hard on a man in this world, boy, if he can't do nothing. If nobody taught him how to use a hammer or a saw, he'll be a beggar all his days. And den dere's rich folk. They got in der mind them and dey children ain't 'pose to work.

Willing to pay sack of dollar bills fer you do the silliest things. Naw... Ain't nothing to gittin' wealthy boy, easy as eating a hunk of your grand-mammy tator pie. Becoming rich, ni that's a mule of a different color."

"A mule of a different color," said Little George, "that's funny granddaddy." Pa-Ty and Little George laughed.

"Giddy up girl!"

"Granddaddy! There's the road to the house." Little George exclaimed.

"How many years me an' Dalla come back in forth on this road? Don't thank we know the way back?" They laughed again.

"This was a long ride granddaddy." Little George observed. "We been gone since before daybreak. Now the sun is about to go in."

"Happen everyday boy, ain't never no different. Gotta git everything done in between. Time more precious than money."

"Granddaddy," Little George asked with a high degree of curiosity, "you take this long ride all the way to the famers market in Augusta every Saturday morning?"

"Yep. Long back as I kin remember. Me and ol' Dalla here." Pa-Ty answered.

"What you gon' do when we git to the house granddaddy or you going to take a nap?" Little George never had seen Pa- Ty laugh so hard and for so long. Pa-Ty laughed until the house was in sight.

Dalla, without any instruction or tap of the strap, turned left just pass the Purdue grocery. Pass the giant white house with the long white columns and balconies in front of the upstairs windows, where the Burke family lived. The red dirt road off Highway 25 was the longest road Little George had ever seen.

He loved to ride down that road watching Uncle Ernest, yellow and white 1958 Buick kick up dust. Uncle Ernest drove really fast down the long red dirt road whenever he brought Little George and his two sisters, Cynthia and Cecelia, and brothers Tyrone and Butch to visit granddaddy.

At the beginning of each summer Little George's momma would put him on the Trailway bus. The bus would stop at the Purdue store. Little George would have to walk down that long hot red dirt road carrying his old brown leather suitcase.

He had enough clothes in it to last the summer through. He would take a few rest stops along the way. There were no trees to stand under. Little George had an old handkerchief to wipe his brow and blow the dust out of his nose. It didn't matter to him though. He was going to granddaddy's house for summer vacation.

Mr. Burke was standing on his porch holding a large iron cup. Little George could see smoke billowing from the chimney. "Hi you been Pa-Ty?" Mr. Burke yelled.

"No complaints su!" Pa-Ty yelled back. "Good Lawd took me and brung me back. Nothing to complain about." "You preaching tomorrow down at the Old Macedonia Baptist Church?" asked Mr. Burke.

"Reckon so, ifn the good Lawd wake me in time."

"You some kinda preacher Pa-Ty!" yelled Mr. Burke. "Me and the wife can hear your members singing and shouting way up here."

"Thank ya, su," Pa-Ty mumbled, "it ain't me su, it whut the good Lawd give me. I ain't nutin' without the good Lawd."

"Have a good supper Pa-Ty," Mr. Burke said. "You too, su."
"Granddaddy," Little George said, "you ain't told me the secret to gittin' rich and we almost to the house."

"The good Lawd give another day tomorrow if n you ask him tonight in yo prayers." Pa-Ty responded.

"Can we talk when we get to the house? I really wanna be rich granddaddy."

Pa-Ty said, "Got work to do." "It's gittin' dark granddaddy."

"Dats what the good Lawd give us the moon fer. Dat don't work, kerosene and fire give us nearly much light as the sun, plus keep yo hands warm. Whoa Dalla, whoa girl."

Little George's stomach was reminding him that he had not eaten since around noon. As soon as Dalla stopped in front of her shed, Little George jumped clear off the wagon and began running toward the house and Grandmamma's kitchen.

Little George knew that on Saturday Grandmamma always cooked a giant pot of field peas with great big hunks of ham from Pa-Ty's smoke house. So many hunks of smoked ham would be in the peas it would be hard to stir the pot.

Little George knew that with peas Grandmamma always made cornbread or fat biscuits, black molasses and her delicious, sweet lemonade. Just the thought nearly drove Little George crazy. Not to mention Grandmamma's tall pound cake. Just before Little George landed from his high jump to the front porch, Pa-Ty's gruff voice froze him in midair. "Where you going boy?"

"Uh, uhh, it supper time, granddaddy. Ain't you coming in to eat?"

"Supper gon' be dar boy. Be waiting right dar fer us after we unhitch Dalla, cool her down wit' water, cover her good with the wool blanket, and make sho' she got plenty supper. Supper be waiting fer us u'all see."

Pa-Ty could see that Little George was really hungry. "Po' folks rush to the supper table boy, fo' the chores done, boy. You do what po' folk do long enough you be one of 'em. You git dat boy?" You wanna be rich among other men in yo' time boy?"

One

becomes

what one

practices.

"Ni git you some water and finish up fo the good Lawd turn the heater completely off out here. Body most need water, mo' than yo grandmammy cooking anyhow."

It took about an hour to take care of Dalla and put the wagon under the shed. Pa-Ty and Little George walked back to the house. Pa-Ty dropped his right arm over Little George's shoulders and pulled him close. They made their way up the hill to the house.

"Granddaddy when I git rich, um gonna pay some body to do my work."

Pa-Ty laughed again. "Rich man do anything he want, ain't never gon' be no different."

"Granddaddy?" Little George asked. "Yep." "You gon' tell me the secrets?"

Pa-Ty smiled. "If 'n the good Lawd wakes us up in the morning and git us to church and back, we can talk during the afternoon and into the night. We git Dalla down to the creek. Take a few baits and poles wit' us, might make the time pay."
"Okay granddaddy." Little George said as the smell of smoked ham drew him toward Grandmamma's kitchen.

CHAPTER 8
Sunday Morning

"Git up boy. Time to git to church everybody ready but you. Bring that dollar I paid ya' yesterday..."

 After that long buggy ride to Augusta and back, Little George would rather do exactly what he would be doing if he were back home in Augusta, instead of at Pa-Ty's house. For a few minutes, he imagined he was at home in his bed that he shared with his younger brother..

Lying on his side under Grandmammas' heavy multicolored quilt, made by her own two hands, Little George closed his eyes for five more long restful moments.

Little George's dream was shattered by Grandmamma's soft voice. "Little George, get up baby. Pa- Ty already on the wagon. Got you a peppermint. Come on my big little man. One day you gonna be rich enough to order granny pretty red dresses."

"Okay Grandmamma," Little George murmured as he yawned and stretched. Little George made a brief stop at the pail of cool water that was on the wooden table in the corner of the back bedroom. In the water was a hunk of homemade lye soap and an old, white rag.

By the time Little George stormed out the front door in his city clothes and onto the porch, all the good seats were taken. Pa-Ty and Grandmamma were sitting up front. Uncle Bosie, Jabo, Buddy, Earnest, and Uncle Jake occupied all the wooden crates in the back of the wagon.

"Ain't" Sallie Mae, "Ain't" Sissy, and Bae were squeezed into the tiny bench right behind Pa- Ty and Grandmamma.

"Where am I going to sit granddaddy," Little George asked, "nowhere for me to sit." "Make room fer dat boy back dare y'all," Pa- Ty said in his deep voice.

"Gotta git going. Be late for my own preaching. Giddy up Dalla!" As she did every Sunday, Dalla patiently and slowly carried Pa-Ty McKie's family to the old Macedonia Baptist

Church without any instructions or directions.

The first thing Little George did after Pa-Ty let church out, was ask Grandrnamma for the peppermint she had promised him. That was the sweetest peppermint candy Little George ever tasted. It lasted all the way back to the Burke plantation.

Just before Little George squeezed from between Uncle Buddy and Uncle Bosie and jumped off the wagon, he said, "Thank you Grandmamma." Grandmamma wiped the sticky peppermint off of his jaw and planted a kiss.

"Grandrnamma, when I git rich um gonna buy me a whole mountain of peppermint." "Rich man buy what he want, gon' always be datta way," said Pa-Ty.

Little George jumped off the wagon and started running toward the edge of the giant peach orchard to play a while with his cousin. "Where you going boy?" Pa-Ty yelled.

"Can I go down by the peach orchard to play?"

"Git back here boy. Rich man ain't got time to play. Playing meant for po folk. Soon as I git outta my church clothes, and you git outta of youm, and Dalla get a rest, We going down to the creek. Time to talk."

"Okay, granddaddy." Little George really wanted to play with his cousins but he was more eager to learn the secrets to riches.

CHAPTER 9
Down at The Old Creek

"Whoa Dalla, whoa girl." Pa-Ty said. "Grab dem poles boy take 'em down to the creek. I ketch up with you after while I reckon, feeling kinda pohly. Good Lawd git me down dere after while I reckon." Little George was born liking fishing.

He quickly gathered the pole and the can of baits and dashed down the dirt path to the creek to wait on Pa-Ty. Pa-Ty took longer than usual to reach the creek on this sunny Sunday afternoon. "What's the matter granddaddy," asked Little George, "you alright?"

"Right as I ever go be I reckon. Been on this ol' Earth 90 years. Can't jump off the wagon like I used to. Gonna keep going though, 'til the good Lawd reach out and throw me in the slave hole and pull me in to be with him and yo great grandpappy and mammy. Ain't never been no different, ain't goanna never be I reckon."

As Pa-Ty used his stick to ease down on his favorite fishing spot, on the ground just at the edge of the creek, Little George noticed what looked like a small watermelon stuffed inside Pa-Ty's overalls down near his private parts. "Granddaddy," Little George murmured, "yo hernia out again?"

Life is cyclical.

"Reckon so," Pa-Ty huffed, "been coming in out for so long I cain't remember when it started. Used to could push it back in. Won't go back no mo'." Little George never seen Pa-Ty this uncomfortable. He got scared, really scared. "Granddaddy?"

"What boy, you ain't got no pole in the water yet?"

"Granddaddy, do Dalla know where the hospital is?" Little George carefully asked.

"Reckon she do." Pa-Ty answered faintly.

"Do you wanna go to the hospital granddaddy?"

"What fer?" Pa-Ty asked. "Been dere so many times I cain't count. Like I told you, they ain't go let me in that hospital. Say um too old ta mess wit. Give me this medicine though. Help the pain some."

"Where does a hernia come from granddaddy?" Little George asked.

"Don't rightly know boy. Dem fellas at the hospital say it come from straining to much. Most all these old sharecroppers got the same thing. Nothin' special about me, I reckon. Grab that pole boy, fo' that catfish take it cross the creek."

Pa-Ty laughed.
"Wow!" Little George screamed, as he wrestled the tiny catfish out the creek. He and Pa-Ty laughed even harder.

Avoid Self-Pity.

CHAPTER 10
Pa-Ty's Seven Wisdoms

Wisdom I:

"Here that dollar back you give me this morning." Little George had forgotten that he gave Pa-Ty his dollar he earned at the farmer's market. He was so happy to get it back. Little George was puzzled when he counted his coins.

Instead of the four coins Pa-Ty gave him at the famers market, Little George counted only two quarters and two dimes. "Granddaddy you lost some of my dollar. Ain't but seventy cents granddaddy."

Little George sounded as if he was going to cry. "You wanna be rich or not boy, or do you wanna be like most these other dirt floor sharecroppers on this here plantation? Ain't worth the salt in de bread! You wanna be like dem folks you saw back in the woods standing round the fire barrel?"

"No sir."

"Listen to me and listen to me good you hear me boy?"

"Yes sir."

"Don't never spend mo' den seventy cent out each dollar you ever git yo hands on. I don't care hi it come to you. Don't ever do it long as you on this here Earth. See this here can boy? Look inside. Whut you see?"

Build your personal economy 70%.

"My other thirty cents." Little George was so happy that the rest of his dollar was there. Pa-Ty reached into the can and pulled out a dime. "Ni dis here go to the preacher, so he go round through dem woods, help dem other po' folks ain't got nuttin', never gonna have nuttin'. I'll keep it, give it to 'em next Sunday.

"Okay." Little George said like a little lost puppy.

"Ni this here two dimes, don't ever take 'em out the can, not ever, less yo wife or chullins sick and need medicine. You got that boy?"

"Yes sir. Granddaddy why do I gotta give a dime to the preacher?" Little George asked.

"Cause the good Lawd said 'do,' I reckon." Pa-Ty replied. "Ain't gotta give it to the preacher I guess, long as the dime git to the po.' Strange thing seem to happen to ya when ya give to the po'. Seem you don't never be po' and the po' fella stay away from yo watermelon patch. If a man any good at all, it just make him feel good to do good. Strangest thing boy."

"So, I can spend the other 70 cents?"

"Spend any sensible way you wanna. Just so wife 'n chullins belly full, ain't no rain or cold gittin' too close to 'em, you ain't in no man debt, got plenty seed for planting, clothes on every body's back, shoes on they feet. Good Lawd take care the rest I reckon. You understand me boy? Promise boy?" Pa-Ty insisted.

"I promise granddaddy ...Granddaddy?" Little George replied.

"Whutboy?"

The poor shall always be with you.

"Why so many people round here po'? Little George asked.

Pa-Ty said, "Ain't never been no different. Never gon be no different."

"The good Lawd give us this here earth and everything in it," Pa-Ty began,"give us everything we could ever need in life. Food, the sun even cook it fer you. Rain fer yo crop and fer drinking. Trees for when the sun git to hot. Fire to warm when it git cold. Ocean full with every kinda fish you kin think of, cain't never eat um all. Nuttin' the good Lawd didn't think of."

"Then why so many people po' granddaddy?" Little George asked curiously, "if God gave us everything?"

"Listen to me boy, dis very important." Pa-Ty barked. "Put that pole down and look at me. The good Lawd give us dis here Earth like I said. Funny thang though, he decided to leave Mama Nature in charge."

"Mother nature." Little George whispered as he scratched his forehead. "Who is Mother Nature?" "She in charge of when the cold wind blow. The rain come. In charge of the pretty flowers and the hurricanes. In charge every thang. Ni boy Mama Nature don't seem to care whut you do wit' whut God give you. Take fire for instance boy, a man kin decide to cook a hog for supper wit' it or use it to burn his house all the way to the ground.

Mama Nature ain't never get in his way. Ain't never go be no different. Member dat dare dog back dare in dem woods, frozen hard as a piece of firewood and covered wit' dem white worms? Don't seem to matter nune to Mama Nature if the dog eat worms or the worms eat the dog. Don't matter nune atall to her. Ain't never go be no different."

Little George didn't like what he heard about Mother Nature being neutral. He thought Mother Nature was mean and cruel.

"Granddaddy?" Little George replied. Pa-Ty huffed, "Whut boy?"

"I don't like Mother Nature." Pa-Ty laughed hard and did not stop until the cantaloupe size swelling in his private area hurt too bad.

"You alright papa? I'm gonna git Dalla and take you to that hospital in Edgefield granddaddy."

"Quit being silly boy. Ain't got much time. You like ya grandma sweet potato pie?

"Yessss, sir!" Little George said and his eyes widened and he rubbed his belly in a circular motion. "Hi dem sweet potatoes git in you grandma pan and in yo belly?" Pa-Ty continued. "You picked dem granddaddy," Little George said.

"Whut wudda happened ifn they didn't git picked from the dirt?" Pa-Ty asked.

"I don't know," Little George answered softly. Pa- Ty barked, "Dey wudda rot in the dirt boy. Make no never mind to Mother Nature. Anything good or bad happen on this here Earth, man cause it. Ain't never go be no different."

"Are you going to go to the hospital granddaddy?" Little George asked again.

"Ain't no need fer it. Told ya dem doctors ain't go spend no time on me. I ain't no mo' good to him. Time close fer me to git throwed down the slave hole wit' my mammy and my pappy. Little George wanted to cry.

pappy. Little George wanted to cry. "Granddaddy, will we get a hospital one day?" Little George pitifully asked. Pa-Ty answered calmy, "Don't know. One day I reckon. Ain't nuttin' but water and cement. Mama nature done give it all to ya. Don't make her no never mind though."

Wisdom III: Don't Go Fishing with One Pole

Little George didn't notice his fishing pole being pulled in the creek. "How you go ketch catfish wit' no pole boy?" Pa-Ty laughed. Little George managed to grab on to his fishing pole just as it reached the edge of the creek.

"Granddaddy, help!" he yelled as the tiny monster catfish insisted on keeping his pole. Pa-Ty, even if he wanted to, could not get up in time to help little George. Besides, he was laughing and enjoying the show too much. Finally, after what felt like hours to Little George, the battle was won.

The tiny monster catfish won and swam away. The catfish looked back at Little George and made a funny face. Little George was clearly angry and disappointed that he lost the battle.

"Whut you all tied up in a knot fer?" Pa-Ty huffed at Little George.

Little George said, "That fish gotta way and took my pole." Little George said with tears in his eyes.

"The good Lawd stuck enough fish in dat creek fer us all boy. Don't never fret over no fish boy. Plenty mo' where dat one come from. It's up to you to git em out."

"But my pole is gone granddaddy." Little George cried out "Reckonso."Granddaddy answered.

"Can I use one of yo poles granddaddy?" Little George begged. "Reckon not." Pa-Ty replied.

Pa-Ty never changed his mind about letting Little George use one of his fishing poles. Instead, he just kept filling his own bucket up with beautiful catfish. Little George looked on with awe, anger, and self-pity. Finally, Little George broke the silence. "Granddaddy?"

"Yea boy?" Pa-Ty absentmindedly answered.

"What's the fastest way for me to git rich? I wanna be rich so I can pay those doctors to take care of you."

"Reckon the fastest way to git rich round here, to go in town and rob dat bank down on Broad Street in Augusta." Pa-Ty chuckled.

"Granddaddy," Little George yelled, "I don't steal!" They both laughed very hard. Pa-Ty said, "You asked for the quickest way, didn't you?"

"Be for real, for real granddaddy," said Little George." I gotta git rich quick so I can get you an operation."

Pa-Ty said very seriously, "Only way to git rich quick is to steal and

rob. Otherwise, it take a little while. Quick money don't last fer some reason though. Besides, how many times I gotta tell you dem doctors ain't gonna operate on me no matter hi much money you give 'em. Say um too old. Aint no use no mo'. I can't plow from sun up to sun down like I used to with hardly a jug of water.

The Law of Diminishing Returns

Dey done with me ni. No good to them. Ain't never gonna be no different. Ain't never been no different. Ain't no man gonna give you a dollar if you can't work fer him."

"Granddaddy?" Little George asked softly. "Whut boy?" Pa- Ty hollered in pain has he grabbed the huge, aching bulge hanging down from his private part. Little George had never heard his granddaddy holler for nothing. He was scared and pretended he didn't hear Pa-Ty's yell. He sat quiet and scared for several minutes.

After a long period of time, Little George sheepishly asked, "Granddaddy, what kind of business should I have to make me lots of the most money fast?" "Hush up boy. Lemme rest fer a minute," Granddaddy said. The bulge was protruding out larger and more painful. "Wanna say dis the right way." Pa-Ty mumbled in pain.

Little George got quiet, just like Pa-Ty told him. After a couple of minutes, Pa-Ty said, softly, "Little George, it don't really matter which business you go into, don't matter atall. Just pick something you wanna do fer folk an' git good at it. Do it fer many folks as you kin. Put the first thirty cents they give you in the tin can. Be rich before you kin say sweet apple pie. If it git too much work fer ya, plenty good fer nuttin' fellas 'round here will help ya for half dollar and drink of whiskey. Gittin' rich the easy part."

"Easy?" Little George asked in amazement. "Lots a folks can't do nothing it seem Pa-ty said. They need everything done for them. Granddaddy?" Little George asked, "you mean I can just pick anything."

"Just about." Pa-Ty answered. "Reckon so. People need help with everything to manage their life. Just pick one thing to help him out, git good at. They make you rich. Fellas these days not like fellas during my pappy days. Your grand pappy and every other fella during his day did everything fer himself and the rich fellas. Built the big houses, cut the firewood, plant and pick the crops in the field. The wife sewed the dresses, did the cooking, most of the praying.

A man did everything fer himself and his family Man even made his own leather shoes for his family. Can't believe how lazy and dumb fellas is these days. Fellas and gals these days can't seem to do very much. They have to git other folks to help skin their own chickens and cook it for them. Pay a dollar for it too. Can't believe my own eyes. Yep," said Pa-Ty, "riches to be got everywhere you look. This is the best time to be alive on this here earth for the fella with a little salt in his bread. Drive you crazy so much money to be made. Gotta know hi do mo' then one thang though," Pa- Ty said. "Mo' thangs a fella know how to do, quicker he git rich. Ain't much to it I reckon."

"Where do I start granddaddy?" Little George asked.
"Do I start fixing wagons fer people or running errands?"
"Don't matter none I told you. Ain't you listening boy?" Pa-Ty said sternly.

"Yes sir, granddaddy."

Pa-Ty went on, "The first thang you gotta do though, before you worry 'bout doing yo business, is figuring out what you believe in or what kinda fella you wanna be known for."
Little George interrupted again, "Whatta you mean granddaddy? What kinda fella: I wanna be known for. What does that have to do with anything?"

"Mean every thang boy. Cain'! git rich without it. No matter how many thangs you know how to do, if folks don't trust you or don't like ya, you can't git no work. Be po' all yo days. A fella with a bad reputation, be po' all his days. Don't matter how many thangs he good at. Your reputation is the most valuable coin in your pocket. After a while, it arrive at the job before you get there. You got that boy?" Pa-Ty bellowed.

"Yes sir, granddaddy... Granddaddy," Little George asked softly, "where can I find a good reputation. Can I use yours granddaddy?"

Pa-Ty laughed until his hernia hurt. "A good reputation can't be found boy. You can't use the other fellas either. Reputation gotta be built over time, one job at a time. Only you can build it." Pa-Ty could see that Little George was a little confused. Pa-Ty took a very deep breath as if to gather the right words.

"Why you think folks, black and white around here, always coming up to your granddaddy for help? "Because you can do everything granddaddy." Little George answered proudly. Pa-Ty laughed softly and said, "That's just half of the coin."

"Half of the coin granddaddy?" Little George asked.
"Yep!" said Pa-Ty.
"What's the other side of the coin granddaddy?" Pa-Ty breathed deeply again. Pa-Ty knew that Little George had to understand this part. He paused for a longer while. Finally, Pa-Ty said, "You ever see a fella, black or white, refuse to give me my dollar after the work done."

"No sir." Little George answered respectfully.

"You ever see a fella, black or white, yell at your granddaddy cause the work was done poorly or not on time?"

Again, Little George respectfully answered, "No sir. Sometimes granddaddy," Little George expressed, "people pay you more money than you ask for. Why do they do that granddaddy?"

"Cause they happy with the job I done, I reckon. Most fellas pay more when the work make them happy. Some fellas are poor pay masters no matter how good the work is done. Don't spend much time thinking about them. Just focus on your own philosophy. Do you get it now boy," Pa-Ty asked, "do you get it?"

"I think so." Little George asked, "Granddaddy?" Pa-Ty exhaled. "Yes son."

"What is a philosophy?"

"Always begin wit' yo philosophy, den yo business." Pa-Ty answered.

Little George repeated the question, "What is a philosophy granddaddy?"

"Yo philosophy is like the power in that mule. It keeps you plowing through the snow and through sun baked clay and mud. It gives you vision when you plow under the stars to git the job done on time. Your philosophy is like that star the preacher preached about First Sunday. Remember that sermon boy?" Pa-Ty grumbled. "Yes sir." Pa-Ty tested Little George. "Tell me about it," he said.

Pa-Ty was surprised with the answer Little George gave. "Those three kings followed a star all the across the giant desert, and never lost their way," Little George said. Pa-Ty laughed loudly and proudly. "Well, I'll be a monkey's uncle!" he expressed. Pa-Ty laughed until the pain stopped him.

"You got it Lil' Bully. You really got it. Your philosophy is just liked that star up in the night sky. The good Lawd put up there so you wouldn't get lost or scared half the death when night fall come while you on yo' journey. The good Lawd seemed to have thought of everything seem like. Ain't nuttin' he didn't think of."

Little George did not want his granddaddy to know he didn't quite understand but it showed on his little dirty face. Finally, he asked, "Granddaddy, what is your philosophy?" Pa-Ty caught his breath that had been taken from him by the pain in his private part, pulled himself up against a tree.

"Reckon I got a bunch of them. Sometimes yo philosophy change on ya. If it ain't working might have to change it. Always gotta have one though. You need at all times or you will find yourself tumbling in whatever direction Mama Nature blows her wind. You will end up at bottom of the hill with nothing to show for it but dusty clothes."

Pa-Ty laughed a short laugh. It hurt too bad to laugh now. The swollen area between his legs was just too painful.

"What's your philosophy?" Little George anxiously asked again.

"Whoa yo mule boy!" Pa-Ty said. "Don't thank you gonna take my philosophy and run cross the field with it. You gotta get your own. Every man with any salt in his bread has his own philosophy."

"I know granddaddy. I just wanna know yours." Little George replied.

"What for?" Pa-Ty gruffed.

"I just wanna know granddaddy!" responded Little George with the face of a curious puppy.

"Well," Pa-Ty pondered, "guess it want spoil you none. My philosophy simple boy. If ain't simple most likely it ain't worth having boy. When a man telling ya the truth, it always come out simple. Take no time to speak what's true, no time at all. Most things can be answered with a quick yes or no.

A fella take more words than that, keep your hand on your money can. Now boy, my whole philosophy can be summed like this: learn how to do many things as you can. Do things for many folks as you can. Do them the very best you can. Do the job you say you are gonna do, when you say you gonna do it. Sell your labor at a fair price.

You can't get rich off of one customer. Don't ever change ya price once you speak it. Always do more for the fella than he pay you for. Do it quicker dan you promise. Don't never take a job too big for you to handle. Never stare into the eyes of your customer's wife or his daughter. Keep your ax sharp, your mule full of water. Always own your own mule.

Use every drop of sun light the good Lawd give you to get done what you promised. Pay your money can before anybody else. Never take nothing outta a man store you can't pay for right on the spot. Best go hungry for a few day 'ti! you can pay for it.

A little hunger never kill no body. Get your rest when the good Lawd turn out his light. Be sitting on porch in the morning waiting for the good Lawd to the tum light back on. Don't ever stop 'ti! they throw ya down the slave hole with me and ya grandmammy and grand pappy.

We'll be waiting on you to show up rich. If you ain't rich, we have to send you back. Ain't never been no different, ain't never go be no different."

Little George was exhausted by time Pa-Ty paused to breathe and grab the painful bulge down in his private parts,

that was hurting so bad. "I gotta do all that in order to git rich granddaddy?" Little George asked.
Pa-Ty said, "Reckon so. Gotta do dat to git rich, gotta do dat to stay rich. No need a being rich just fer a few days."

"Wow!" Little George gasped.

Pa-Ty suddenly laughed again. "Like I said before, you kin just ride down to Augusta and rob the bank. Mama nature ain't go put nuttin' in yo' way to try and stop ya!" Little George and Pa-Ty grabbed each other and laughed.

"As I said boy, don't never forget, gittin' rich is easy. What kinda fella you end up being while you gittin" rich is what count." Finally, the laughing stopped and silence returned. Little George asked, "Granddaddy, why you gotta own your own mule granddaddy?"

Pa-Ty laughed a little more. "If a man ain't got no mule, he can't git to de field for plowing, got nuttin' to hitch his plow to when he git dare. A fella ain't got his own mule, never be much mo' than a boy. He gotta wait standing on the porch until the boss man come git him and take him to field.

Boss man have to give him everything he need to work with. Po' fella ain't even got no place to hide his biscuits. The boss most likely gotta feed him too. Is that the kinda fella you wanna be Lil' Bully?" Pa-Ty gave little George the nickname when he was born.

"No sir granddaddy," Little George said, "I'm gonna always own my own mule granddaddy. I'm gonna own a thousand mules." Pa-Ty laughed harder than he ever had in all his days. "Another thang I tell ya boy."

"What is that granddaddy?" Little George asked.

Pa-Ty looked seriously into Little George's eyes, maybe for the first time ever. "A man who own his own mule will get rich quicker than a man standing on the porch or beside the dusty road waiting on the boss to give him a ride to the field."

"Why is that granddaddy?" Little George asked.

Pa-Ty paused a bit, took a deep breath, tried to pushed the swelling in his pants back up into his gut to ease the pain.

"There is two types a sharecroppers Lil' Bully." "Two types, granddaddy?"

"Yes," Pa-Ty said. "There is a three-dime sharecropper and a five-dime sharecropper." Little George was clearly puzzled. Pa-Ty said, "Fella who ain't got much sense in his head oughta be able to figure that a fella who get paid five dimes for his labor will end up rich before the fella who don't earned but three dimes for the same work. That don't take no sense at all."

"How many dimes do you get granddaddy?" Little George asked as they begin loading up for the ride back home. Pa- Ty proudly answered, "I earned five dimes outta each dollar me and old Dalla can dig out the earth the good Lawd give us.

"Wow," said little George. "Five dimes?" "Yep!" Pa-Ty replied.

"Is that why you got so many hams in your smoke house?

You own your own cow for milking too?" Little George asked.

"Reckon so." Pa-Ty quietly answered. "Granddaddy?" Little George said.

Pa-Ty was growing tired. "Yea Lil' Bully?"

"Who gets the other five dimes?" asked Little George. Pa- Ty laughed softly and said, "The landowner gets the rest. We make an even swap at harvest time."

"Is that man that's always standing on that high porch watching his children play in their church clothes the landowner granddaddy?"
Pa-Ty said, "Yep, that's old man Burke. Been knowing him practically since he born."

"Granddaddy, why do you give Mr. Burke the other five dimes? He don't ever get off his horse when he rides through the field. I wouldn't give him any of my dimes, granddaddy," Little George said. Things got a little quiet between Little George and Pa-Ty for a few minutes.

Pa-Ty knew that it was very important that he gave Little George an answer that would clear up his confusion. He could see that Little George was confused and angry about old man Burke receiving five dimes for doing no work at least as far as Little George could see.

Finally, Pa-Ty grumbled, "You wanna be rich boy?" "Yes sir," Little George answered sheepishly, "I wanna be the richest man in the world granddaddy."

"If that be the case then when you make a deal with a man you keep your end of it. No matter what it look like, feel like, are taste like. Don't matter none if it's raining, snowing, or the sun burn a hole in your back. Still get the plowing and the picking done just the way you promise. Good Lawd will get you through it. Pay off in the end."

"But it ain't fair granddaddy!" Little George cried out in frustration. "It ain't fair!"

Pa-Ty chuckled a little and asked Little George, "What part ain't fair Iil' Bully?" Little George cried· out in disgust, "None of it, granddaddy!" Pa- Ty was clearly getting a little irritated. He turned to little George and said angrily, "Ain't but one deal ever been fair since the good Lawd made the world boy."

"What is that granddaddy?" Little George asked quietly. Pa-Ty chuckled again and said, "Good Lawd give every man the same soil, the same rain, sunshine, and seed. Every morning the good Lawd give each fella the same 24 hours to work with as he please.

Left Mama Nature around to make sho' each season come when they supposed to. Sound pretty fair to me boy. Ain't never been no different, ain't never gonna be no different. Some fella own the land, another fella work land. Up to every fella to do what he please with the 24 hours the good Lawd give him each morning. Besides, all the hard work was already done before man first got here."

"What do you mean?" Little George asked. "Good Lawd taken care just about everything. All a fella gotta do is drop a seed in the ground and walk away. Good Lawd water it for him and cook it for him too. Crop be ready to eat in just a few days. That don't sound pretty fair to you Lil' Bully?"

Little George remained quiet. Pa-Ty continued to preach. "If a fella end up with a bad deal at the end of the day, ain't got nobody to holler at but himself. His predicament don't seem to bother Mama Nature none at all. Gittin' rich oughta be the easy thing in the world to do with all the good the good Lawd already done for ya."

Little George was quiet for a while, and then he asked innocently, "Granddaddy?" he paused a moment. "If gittin' rich is so easy, why so many people hungry and po' like those people living back up in the woods standing around the fire barrel? They didn't even have a door on their house granddaddy. Why they want get rich like you, granddaddy?"

"All kinds a reasons, Lil' Bully," said Pa-Ty. "The good book say po' fellas will always be around, didn't say why though. Your job is to not become one of them. You got that Lil' Bully?" Little George suddenly got excited again.

"It's gonna be easy for me to be the richest man in the world granddaddy he yelled!" Pa-Ty said, "Yep, easy as eating a hunk of your grand mammy peach pie." They both laughed. "Remember one thang though Lil' Bully," Pa-Ty said gently.

"What's that granddaddy?" Little George asked. "Any thang easy to do, easier not to do. Don't make no never mind to Mama Nature none at all. Lots a fellas po' all their days simply because it's easier being poor." Little George was quiet again and confused.

"Time to head back to the house Lil' Bully." Pa-Ty announced. "We got enough catfish for supper. Less leave some for the next fella. Don't have to be greedy to be rich Lil' Bully."

"Okay granddaddy," Little George replied. Pa-Ty reached his right arm up toward Little George. "Help me get up boy. Don't know how long the good Lawd gonna keep me on this old Earth. I'm ready to go whenever he say." Little George said very softly, "Don't say that granddaddy."

"Hurt every day boy," Pa-Ty exhaled, "I ain't giving up boy, just giving out...You know the difference, don't you Lil' Bully?" Little George was quiet again. Helping Pa-Ty to his feet was harder than usual. Little George strained and strained, however, until Pa-Ty made it to his feet.

Little George wrapped Pa-Ty's left arm over his shoulder and wrapped his right arm around Pa-Ty's waist. One painful step after the other, finally they arrived at the wagon. Old Dalla, Pa-Ty's devoted lead mule was patiently waiting.

"Giddy up gal." Pa-Ty huffed softly. Pow, pow with the whip, and off Dalla strutted taking her sweet time as usual. The first few minutes of the ride home was quiet. It took Pa-Ty a while to get comfortable. He asked Little George to take the reins and the whip. Little George for the first time felt like a rich man.

"Giddy up Dalla!" he yelled. Pa-Ty laughed until the pain down in his private parts became unbearable. Little George had never heard Pa-Ty or any other man scream. Pa-Ty's pain eased after a while and he was able to sit up and talk again. "Lil' Bully?"

"Yes, granddaddy?" Little George said.

"It's important that you know the difference."

"The difference in what granddaddy?" Little George asked.

Pa-Ty repeated, "The difference between being wealthy and being rich."

Little George answered, "It ain't no difference granddaddy, is it?"

"It's a big difference." Pa-Ty said softly. "It is easy to become wealthy. The truth is, any fella can become wealthy if n he wanna. Just like I said back yonder, all a fella gotta do is learn to fix something. Keep doing it poorly until he get good at it, then go around do it for as many folks as he can. If he throw three dimes in his can outta every dollar that come to him, he will need a bigger can before too long. Ain't nothing hard about that is it boy?"

"No sir." Little George said, still confused.

Pa-Ty went on, "It ain't never go be no different. Ain't nuttin' hard 'bout it."

"Soo, soo, what's the difference granddaddy? Between being rich and being wealthy? Money is money ain't it, granddaddy?" Little George asked.

"Yep," Pa-Ty responded as he adjusted the knot in his private parts and changed his sitting position. "A dollar is a dollar, don't matter if it's Saturday or Sunday, in yo pocket or mine, still a dollar."

"Soooo, what's the difference?" Little George asked again.

"Wealth ain't nothing but dimes in your can. Easy throwing dimes in your can. Rich is something different though," Pa- Ty said.

"Rich is a taste. A taste ain't got much to do with how many dimes in your can. Rich is like a pile of your grand mammy lemon and chocolate pudding, pile on top of her tall pound cake. No matter how many cans of dimes under your bed, you can't buy taste like that."

All little George could think of for the next few seconds was his grandmother's lemon chocolate pudding and pound cake which was his favorite desert in the entire world.

After a while, Little George said, "People gotta taste, granddaddy?"

"Every man got one rather he want it not." Little George was really confused now and Pa-Ty could easily tell. "You done got confused Lil' Bully?" Pa - Ty asked softly.

"Yes sir." Little George managed to squeak out.

"I was afraid that might happen," Pa-Ty said. "Truth is just like medicine, a fella can't take too much at one time, 'less it drive him crazy." Pa-Ty laughed again. The pain from the hernia stopped the laughter.

After the pain settled back down a bit, Pa- Ty said to Little George, "It's like this boy, the good Lawd gave everything he put on this here Earth a taste, including man. Just like them peaches out here in the orchard. A man ain't no different." Pa- Ty could tell by Little George's facial expression he was still not understanding the logic.

Pa-Ty pondered a few minutes, and then asked Little George, "What do your grand mammy do with the sweet peaches from the orchard?"

This was an easy question for Little George.

He loved to help his grandma Nannie mix her cakes pies and puddings. "She put them in her cobbler and pies," he answered, proudly. Little George rubbed his tummy and licked his lips and went, 'uumm,' as the rich taste of his grandmothers' peach pies burst into his memory.

Then Pa-Ty asked, "What does she do with the bitter peaches?"
"She throw them in a slop bucket for the hogs. "Little George said.

Pa-Ty said, "A man ain't no different. Sweet ones go into pies, bitter ones get thrown in the slop bucket sooner or later. It don't matter how many cans a man fill up with dimes and push under his bed. If he leaves a bad taste in the mouth of folks he doing business with, including his neighbors, friend and family, he will soon end up in the slop bucket of life."

Pa-Ty laughed softly. Little George laughed as well.

But Little George was still just a little confused. "How can you taste a man and tell whether he is sweet or bitter?" Little George asked. "Do you just walk up to him and bite a plug out of his arm like grand mama do her peaches?" Pa-Ty laughed harder than he had all day. Even though his hernia was swollen, huge, and was so painful. He just laughed through the pain. "That's one way to tell I reckon," Pa-Ty said, as he kept bouncing and laughing. Little George laughed too.

When Pa-Ty finally stopped laughing, he said, "I guess I'm gonna have to paint a clearer picture inside that thick skull of yours."

"How are you going to do that granddaddy?" Little George asked. Both of them laughed again. Pa-Ty stopped for a while. Finally, Pa-Ty said, "You know ol' man Burke that live in that tall white house your uncles and me built for him? You know the one with the balcony and the giant windows?"

"Yes sir, I know Mr. Burke granddaddy." Little George replied.

"It took us nearly a whole year to build it for him," Pa-Ty recalled.

"Wow, that's a long-time granddaddy!" Little George said. Pa-Ty said, "If you wanna be rich boy, always take your time and do the job better than the next fella can."

"Mr. Burke is so funny! I like to play with his little girls and little Phillip, they are my friends."

"Just let that picture I just painted for you dance around in your head for a few seconds," Pa-Ty said. Little George closed his eyes with the image of him playing tag at the Burke plantation with little Phillip Burke and his three sisters.

The picture in his head painted a giant smile on his face. Little George loved Mrs. Burke's lemonade as much as he loved his grandma nannies'. Pa-Ty asked Little George, "You also know old man Tillman, don't you?" Pa-Ty gruffed.

Little George became quiet for a second or two, and said with a tone of sadness and fear, "He lives in that giant yellow house where the porch sit real high."

Pa-Ty nodded. "He is always sitting up there in his white rocking chair looking out over his cotton fields and-peach orchard and all his pickers. You ever see him smile or laugh?"

"No sir."

"You ever see him hug his children or give Mrs. Tillman a flower?"

"No sir."

"Do you ever stop by and play with his children?" Pa-Ty asked.

"No way," Little George answered, "no way!" "Why not?" granddaddy Pa-Ty asked.

Little George grew eager, "Don't nobody go near Mr. Tillman granddaddy, nobody. He don't even let his children play outside in the front yard. They are always in the back of the house, sitting around in their Sunday clothes. They wear Sunday clothes everyday granddaddy! Mr. Tillman's pickers never look at his face when he rides his horse through the fields granddaddy."

Pa-Ty asked, "Do his madam ever smile at you when she pass by you down at the market?"

"No way granddaddy. Most people even cross the street when they see her and Mr. Tilman coming."

"Are you beginning to see the picture I'm trying to paint in that head of yours?" Pa-Ty asked Little George.
"Yes sir," Little George said softly.

"It is very important that you see this picture crystal clear, Lil' Bully."

Little George answered somberly, "Okay, granddaddy."

"I ain't gonna say it but one time, and one time only. Even if that skull of yours is thicker than an oak tree, you still should see the picture by now." Little George and his Pa-Ty laughed. Pa-Ty, in a rare moment of outward affection, pulled Little George close to him and kissed his forehead. Little George wiped the kiss away. They both laughed.

After a few seconds of silence, Pa-Ty spoke in a gentle voice. "Lil' Bully, a fellas' wealth ain't nothing but cans filled with dimes under his bed. Any fella with just a tiny bit of salt in his bread, can become wealthy with no effort at all.

Wealth alone ain't nothing but rusty dimes in a rusty tin can hidden under the bed. Becoming rich, now that is a horse of a different color." Little George and Pa-Ty laughed together.

Little George suddenly blurted out, "Granddaddy I am gonna have a thousand tin cans filled with dimes under my bed. A million granddaddy!" Pa- Ty replied softly, "But are you gonna become rich as you become wealthy son? It is your granddaddy heart's desire that you become rich along the way to becoming wealthy. Otherwise, I'd rather see you be poor all your days."

Little George was shocked to hear his granddaddy say those words. He was silent for a while. Finally, Little George asked his Pa-Ty, "What is rich granddaddy?" Pa-Ty did not want to lose this moment of opportunity.

There was a long pause. Pa-Ty turned to little George and said, "Rich is that kiss I planted on your forehead. Becoming a rich man has very little to do with how many cans of dimes are hidden under a fellas' bed. Rich is what the fella becomes on the road to becoming wealthy. It is what kind of man you become that makes the big difference Lil' Bully."

Little George thought about what Pa-Ty said for a while. He finally murmured, "So granddaddy, are you saying that Mr. Burke is rich and Mr. Tillman, he is just wealthy? Is that why nobody likes to be near Mr. Tillman?"

"Do you see the difference now boy?" Pa-Ty asked proudly. Suddenly, Little George screamed with excitement, "Granddaddy can I be rich and wealthy?"

Pa-Ty laughed again very, very hard and said happily, "You got it Lil' Bully," Pa-Ty said, "Now you, and ol' Dalla, can take me down to the woods and throw me down the slave hole to be wit' my mammy and my pappy. You got it now boy. You really got it Lil' Bully."

Little George was so happy and proud that he had made Pa-Ty happy. Little George gave Dalla a soft pat with the whip and ordered, "Giddy up gal, giddy up!"

Pa-Ty wrapped his left arm around Little George's body and squeezed him until Little George could hardly breathe. They laughed and they laughed. Little George started to sing, "I'm gonna be rich, I'm gonna be rich, I'm gonna be the richest man in the world!" They both laughed again and Little George got squeezed again.

"You just passed the road that will take us down in the woods, to the slave hole," Pa-Ty said, "my job done now."

Little George said, "Granddaddy, your grandson gonna be the richest man on God green Earth, you ain't going down in no slave.hole. I'm gonna build you your own hospital just like the one down in Augusta, Georgia. Are you happy about that granddaddy?"

"I reckon so." Pa-Ty answered. "A hospital ain't no good though if n ain't no doctor inside willing to lay hands on ya." They both laughed. Pa-Ty said, "I'm just fine the way I am.

The good Lawd done kept me here near 90 years with no doctoring. He kept me here long enough to teach you the secret. He can take me any time he ready for me. Ain't never go be no different." Little George became quiet again for about a mile. "Granddaddy," he asked, "is the slave hole real? Is it really real? I mean for real."

"Sho' it is," said Pa-Ty. "You can't git to heaven to be wit' the good Lawd except you go through slave whole. I never known a fella to leave here walking once the good Lawd called him. Every fella go back to the dirt till the good Lawd lift him up. Ain't never been no different. Ain't never gonna be no different."

"Granddaddy," little George asked fearfully, "did you throw my great grandmother and great granddaddy down the slave hole?"

"Nope." Pa-Ty answered. "Who did granddaddy?"

"I don't know exactly. Doing those days fellas and gals worked till they got too old or too sick to go to the field. Then, they just lay down and die. Sometimes they die in the house. Sometimes they take the last breath in the field.

Don't make no never mind, dead is dead. After the picking git done, the landowner let a couple of fellas take them down in woods throw um down the whole to be wit' they mammy 'npappy and the good Lawd. Ain't never been no diffcrcnt."

Little George began to feel sad. "Granddaddy," he asked, "did my great granddaddy and mama have a funeral?"

"Rich man git funerals and flowers and a stone with his name chipped into it. Po' man git thrown down the hole. Ain't never gonna be no different, less a fella make it different. Mama nature don't seem to mind either way. Don't make her no different atall."

Little George suddenly yelled to Dalla, "Whoa girl, whoa girl!"

"Whut you doing, Lil' Bully?" Pa-Ty yelled. "The house just down the road. You can see it if you look hard enough." Little George looked at Pa- Ty sadly, and said, "Granddaddy?"

"Whut Lil' Bully?" Pa-Ty answered.

"I don't like the story about the slave hole."

Granddaddy replied, "Truth ain't always pretty Lil' Bully," Pa-Ty said. Not many fellas can take too much truth. Truth drive 'em crazy."

"But granddaddy, you told me to never tell a lie cause only truth can set you free."

"I still stand by that," Pa-Ty said. "Only a coward lies.

Telling the truth is mo' complicated." Pa-Ty could see the confusion on Little George's face. "Truth is like medicine and whiskey Lil' Bully."

"Like medicine and whiskey?" Little George chuckled.

"Yep, just like medicine and whiskey." Pa-Ty answered. "Too much medicine, make a fella sick enough to wish he was dead. Too much whiskey make a fella meaner than a wild hog. Truth work the exact same way. Don't ever let a fella scare you so bad that you lie to him. Be just as careful who you share the truth with.

Don't you worry none any way. You ain't never gonna be put in the slave hole. Remember, you gonna be the richest man in the world." Pa- Ty and Little George laughed again.

Little George said, "Granddaddy, who is buried in that field in the middle of downtown in Augusta?"

Pa-Ty asked, "You mean the ones in the middle of broad street? The ones with the big tall stones that climb thirty feet into the sky?"

"Yes, sir." Little George answered softly. "The ones with all those pretty flowers like in the garden of Eden."

"Rich folks buried there. Rich fella gets buried where ever he want to. If a fella ain't got nothing while he living, he ain't gonna get nothing when he dead. That is 'less he ends up in the arms of the good Lawd. Ain't never go be no different, 'less a fella make it different."

Little George gleefully said, "I'm gonna make it different granddaddy. You ain't going down no slave hole. I'm gonna be the wealthiest and the richest man in the whole wide world granddaddy." Pa-Ty said, " Ain't nothing hard bout to gittin" wealthy boy. Just like I told ya back yonder, fellas these days can't do much a nothing. They can't even build his house for his own family. Ain't worth the salt in their bread.

A fella come along know how to build a house, or make a pair shoes, or fix a plow, can fill up his money can so fast make yo head swim. Trick is to get rich while you gittin' wealthy. No need a having your money can filled to the brim if yo family and your neighbors can't stand be around you. It will be just you and yo money can. Got that boy," Pa-Ty barked, "you got that?"

"I got it granddaddy." Little George said. "I'm gonna be wealthy and rich granddaddy."

Pa-Ty reached around Little George's body and squeezed again until Little George couldn't breathe. "Now git Dalla to stepping. We gotta drop these here catfish before your grand mammy grease get cold."

Little George gave Dalla a gentle pop of the whip and she began her slow steady pull toward the Burke plantation. "Giddy up girl!" Little George, Pa-Ty, and Dalla just slowly and happily headed for home.

"Whoa Dalla!" Little George yelled as they arrived in front of the sharecropper shack. "Whoa girl." Uncle Buddy, Uncle Bosie, Aunt Sallie Mae, and Little George's mama, Moriah, were all standing on the porch waiting for Pa-Ty and Little George to return with the catfish for supper.

Grand mama Nannie was inside the kitchen stirring the collard greens and pork meat and making sure the com bread didn't burn in the black iron pot belly stove. Three peach pies were cooling in the window. The smell of the peach pies was so delicious, Little George jumped off the wagon before Dalla even came to a complete stop. He landed hard, fell down, and rolled about three times.

Everybody laughed and chuckled, including Pa-Ty. It was a rare sight for Pa-Ty's sons and daughters to see him smile, they were shocked. Little George didn't mind the laughing the only thing on his mind was gittin' to his Grandma Nannie's peach pies.

Pa-Ty yelled as he kept laughing, "Git back here boy! You help your granddaddy get off this here wagon! You wouldn't have to worry 'bout me if you had dropped me down the slave hole like I told." Everybody laughed. Little George returned to the to the wagon and did his best to help Pa-Ty climb down from the wagon. Uncle Buddy and uncle Bosie realized that Pa- Ty was in pain. They jumped off the porch to help.

It appeared that the cantaloupe size bulge down in Pa-Ty's private parts was now the size of a watermelon. Little George noticed that the bulge was now twice as large as it was before. He became really scared.

"Let's take granddaddy to the hospital!" Little George yelled to his uncles and aunts standing around the porch. No one responded, just looked down toward the ground.

"Hush up Lil' Bully," Pa-Ty barked. "They ain't gonna do no doctoring on no old run-down sharecropper near 90 years old. No mo' good to um." Pa-Ty mumbled in pain. "Hospital for rich fellas."

"But granddaddy, you are rich!" Little George cried out. "You are the richest sharecropper in Edgefield County. You got enough to feed all those poor people living back in the woods. You own two mules and you even got a milk cow and granddaddy, I peeked under yo bed, all your cans are filled with silver coins." Little George felt completely helpless and afraid.

Pa-Ty said weakly, "Boy a fella money ain't no good if the next fella don't want it. They ain't gonna let me in that hospital even if I pulled up with that dare wagon loaded down with silver and gold." Pa- Ty managed to get out a laugh through the pain.

Little George looked again towards his elders on the porch and they again looked to the ground. A tear began to form in the corner of Little George's eyes. Again, Little George looked up towards the porch, with tears in his eyes and said, "Do something." He was met with complete silence.

Pa-Ty noticed that Little George was crying. . "Them tears in your eyes Lil' Bully?" Pa-Ty's voice bellowed like an angry lion. Little George tried to wipe the tears away quickly' but they were quickly replaced with more. "Boy I been wasting my time with you, haven't I? Telling you all the secrets to becoming a man of wealth and riches. Have I?"

Pa-Ty screamed at Little George, as he grabbed the huge mass hanging between his legs. "If I ever see a tear in your eye caused by another fella doing what he please with what he got, you gonna feel that whip that's tied to the back of this here wagon. Do hear me boy?"

Little George's sadness was replaced with fear. He had seen Pa-Ty use that whip whenever his uncles refused to get out of bed and head to the fields on time or after a night of drinking. "Do you hear me boy?" Pa-Ty roared again.

"Yes sir," Little George whimpered, while shaking like a leaf in the wind. "Now y'all help git me in the house and quit making a fuss." Little George did everything he could to assist Pa-Ty into the house and to his favorite chair.

After Pa-Ty managed to catch a breath, he yelled out to Little George, "Don't forget to cool Dalla down and give her plenty water and unhook her from the wagon before you place her in the shed. Rich man don't leave nothing til' tomorrow."

"Okay Granddaddy." Little George responded sadly.

When Little George returned to the house from the mule shed, Pa-Ty had fallen asleep in his chair. Little George noticed several empty packs of Goody headache powder and a bottle of pills sitting on the old three-legged light brown wooden table that always was next to Pa-Ty's chair. It held Pa-Ty's water jar and tobacco can. Grandmamma Nannie dropped the catfish in the grease. Little George could hear the popping sound coming from the kitchen. He could smell the wonderful aroma all the way to the porch.

Little George walked into the kitchen where Grandmamma Nannie was. Grandmamma Nannie knew he was upset. She wiped the flour off of her hands with her red checkered apron. She gave Little George a wonderful hug. "Grandmamma?" Little George called out.

"Yes, Little George." Grandmamma answered softly and gently.

"What's the matter?" she asked. Little George paused nervously. Finally, he asked Nannie, "What's wrong with granddaddy? Why won't he let y'all take him to the hospital?"

Grandmamma Nannie wiped her hands again with her apron. She pulled out two of the cherry wood chairs from the table and softly pushed him into one of them. Grandmamma Nannie was quiet for a second or two. "Little George," she said, "your Pa-Ty has what the doctor call a hernia."

"A hernia?" Little George asked. "Yes, a hernia."

"What is a hernia Grandmamma and how did granddaddy got one? Why can't he go to the hospital?" Little George wanted to know.

Grandmamma Nannie said, "Hush up now. Don't talk so loud or you will wake up Pa-Ty. He will have a fit if he finds out I'm telling you this. He will say I'm making you a sissy." "I ain't no sissy Grandmamma!" Little George expressed angrily. Little George held up his fist to show Grandmamma how big it was. Grandmamma laughed. "You'll mess boy." she said.

"What is a hernia?" Little George asked again.

"Now, I ain't no doctor but I'm told that a hernia like..."
Grandmamma Nannie paused as she searched her brain
for the right words. "You know that ball you got out
there under the house?"

"Yes ma'am." Little George nodded his head.

"Why is it under the house and why you don't play
with it anymore?"

"That ball has a split in it Grandmamma." Little George
answered with high curiosity. "The rubber is bursting
through the cover. It won't bounce." Little George
explained.

"Well," Grandmamma Nannie said, "just like that ball of
yours gotta split in it."

"Granddaddy got a split on his intestines. Grandaddy
daddy got a hole in his intestines!!!

"Yes, Little George. And that large bulge you see are his
intestines protruding through the split, just like the inner
tube is protruding through the split on your basketball."

"Oh my God!" Little George said as he covered his
mouth with the palm of his hand. The image
Grandmamma Nannie's words were creating inside of
Little George's brain was making him sick and sad.

"That's right," Grandmamma Nannie said. "That is
what's wrong with Pa-Ty." It took Little George a few
minutes to comprehend what he had just heard from
Grandmamma. When he collected his thoughts he asked,

"How did granddaddy get a hernia Grandmamma?"

She answered, "80 years behind the plow?"

"Is the slave hole real?"

"I'm afraid so, Little George," Grandmamma Nannie answered softly.

CHAPTER 11
Two Hours Later

Little George and all of his cousins were outside playing tag. Grandmamma stood out to the comer of the wooden porch and yelled "Supper ready!" That's the only thing that could stop the tag game in its track.
"Get to the bowl and wash up before you come in my kitchen!" Grandmamma Nannie yelled. By the time Little George and his cousins finished washing up and made it back to the table,

Pa-Ty was already sitting at the head of the old wooden table, which was covered in a red and white plastic checkered table cloth. He had his white cloth stuck down the top of his shirt to keep the grease from the catfish off his overalls.

Little George wondered where Pa-Ty's pain had gone. He tried to see if the hernia was still protruding through his overalls. He couldn't see though because Pa-Ty's legs were too far under the table.

"Let us all bow our head to say grace... ," Pa-Ty ordered. The quiet before Pa-Ty began saying the blessing lasted a bit too long for Little George. He peeked open his left eye to see what was keeping him from Grandmamma Nannie's catfish. Little George kept his head bowed and both hands clasped together under his chin.

"Thank ye good Lawd fer us all gathered round this here table again. Thank you for covering the table with good food and butter milk. Thank ye fer the pond and fish that gathered. Thank ye fer soil and de rain and da sunshine that bring the vegetables fer the table. Thank ye fer giving me and my boys the strength to plow and pick 'em. Ya give us all we need and mo', good Lawd, don't need nuttin' else. Ye so good Lawd. Please bless the hands that cooked the supper. Amen."

That final request always brought a smile to Grandmamma Nannie's face. Little George snuck another peek, just to see Grandmamma Nannie standing next to Pa-Ty. She had her hands folded together at her waist. She had a smile on her face that reminded little George of the angels in his dreams.

Wasn't long before everyone at the table could see the bottom of their plates. Even the saucers that held the pound cake and canned peaches were empty. The lemonade glasses were empty as well. No one would dare, however, leave the supper table before being dismissed by Pa-Ty.

Finally, Pa- Ty said, "From de looks of these empty plates and jars, supper over. Lil' Bully hi bout help ya grand mammy clear the table. When ya done come out to the shed have a little talk with me and old Dalla gal." Little George, Uncle Buddy, and Uncle Bosie, hurried over to help Pa-Ty get up from the table. It was clear to little George that Pa-Ty's pain had return.

Little George hurried to help Grandmamma Nannie clear the table so he could get out to the shed to talk with his beloved granddaddy and his lead mule Dalla. Little George could never get enough of hearing his granddaddy talk about the secrets to wealth and riches.

He could just never get enough. Uncle Buddy hoisted Pa-Ty upward by placing his giant hand under his left shoulder. Uncle Bosie did the same maneuver under Pa -Ty's right shoulder. Pa-Ty used both of his sunbaked leathery hands to push down on the old wooden kitchen table.

Okay, I can make it ni. Jest hand me my stick and git out my way!" Pa-Ty barked. "Come join me Lil' Bully, soon as your grandmammy get through with ya."

"Okay, granddaddy," Little George said. Pa-Ty steadied himself with his stick. Buddy and Bosie carefully backed away as Pa-Ty had demanded. Both of them walked close behind him as he made his way out of the back kitchen door and down the rickety old wooden steps towards the shed.

Somehow, he made it without falling, just like always. Little George could see his granddaddy struggle toward the mule shed by standing on his tippy toes and looking through the window. The window was a large square opening his granddaddy had sawed through the wall over the iron potbellied stove in order for Grandmamma Nannie to feel the breeze from outside while she cooked.

There was a wooden door attached that could be closed and hooked at night or whenever the breeze turned to winter, cold, or rain. Little George watched as Pa-Ty took every wobbly step. He could not wait until his Grandmamma Nannie released him from his chores so he could join Pa- Ty and Dalla out in the old wooden shed. He watched as Pa-Ty disappeared through the opening of the shed.

His freedom came finally. "Ok, Little George," Grandma Nannie said, "go on out there with your granddaddy before you have a fit right here in my kitchen."

Before Nannie could even finish saying kitchen, Little George was in midair jumping off the back porch headed for the shed. When Little George arrived at the shed door, Pa-Ty was sitting on the hay covered dirt floor.

He was propped up against a large bale of hay as he often was. He was pushing hands full of hay into Dalla's's mouth. Dalla was clearly enjoying her supper and Pa-Ty was equally enjoying serving her.

"Come on in here Lil' bully and fetch ol' Dalla gal here some water. A rich man don't never turn in for the night until his mule is fed and watered. He won't be rich long ifn he do." Little George was happy to get water for Dalla. He loved Dalla as much as Pa-Ty did. After placing the water bucket so Dalla could enjoy it

Little George flopped down on a bale of hay right next to Pa-Ty. They just sit there for a long while and just enjoyed Dalla slurping her precious water.

Little George's eyes of course could not stop staring at the huge hernia bulge pressing through his granddaddy's overalls. He didn't dare say a word. He just kept staring and wondering. Pa-Ty didn't seem to be bothered by his staring at all.
"Lil' Bully," Pa-Ty said, interrupting Little George's thoughts.

Little George jumped a little, awaken from his gaze.

"Yes, granddaddy?"

"I got a couple mo' secrets to share with you and now is as good a time as ever."

"Okay granddaddy." Little George was ready.

"What I'm gonna tell ya could be a great help to ya, or it could be a burden, depending on how you use it boy."

"Yes, sir granddaddy," Little George answered.

"You and me been talking a lot about building wealth and riches for a long time. I done told you practically every thang you will ever need to know. Soon you gonna be just like these big shot landowners. Like these rich fellas riding around here on their pretty horses. There ain't nothing to it really."

"What you going to tell me now granddaddy?" Little George was really excited. "I already know everything I gotta do to get rich granddaddy," Little George said.

Pa-Ty smiled and asked little George, "How you gonna get rich Lil' Bully?"

Little George said, "All I gotta do granddaddy, is learn how to do lots of things just like you. Make shoes outta cow hide, plant and plow the fields, build houses and barns and do them for lots a people."

"And what you gonna do with every dollar your customer give to you for the work you done for him?"

Little George smiled proudly and said, "Drop three dimes in my can take out one fer the preacher. Use de rest as I please." Pa-Ty laughed and laughed 'til the pain came back. Pa-Ty finally stopped laughing. "You forgot a few things Lil' Bully." Pa- Ty pulled Little George close.

Little George thought he had got it all. "What granddaddy? What did I forget?"

Pa-Ty said, "Before a wealthy man get to the do as he please with his money, he first gotta make show his wife got food in her kitchen, clothes on her back and a pretty dress, hat, and shoes to wear for Sunday preaching. All the bellies in the house gotta be full before going to bed at night.

Every foot in the field gotta have cow hide under them for plowing. They gotta have a shiny pair for Sunday. The children gotta have rags on their backs, don't matter how many. All the holes in the roof gotta be patched.

Cain 't no man be searching for you about money you owe him." Pa-Ty whispered. "Once you got that taken care of, along with whatever tricks Mama Nature decide to play on you, you can do whatever you please with what's left. You got that boy?"

Little George was overwhelmed but he smiled and said, "I got it granddaddy." Pa-Ty was pleased. He said, "Little

George with that plan you gonna make you and your wife and chullin a mighty good living. You gonna be rich all your days." Little George was so happy. He wanted to hear more.

"What else is there granddaddy?" he asked.

Pa-Ty answered, "Well, since you gonna be rich, might as well make you a fortune."

"What is a fortune granddaddy?" Little George asked eagerly.

Pa-Ty smiled and said, "A fortune is having mo' money than you can keep under the bed. More money than you or anybody can ever count."

"Wow! That's a lotta money granddaddy. How can I get me a fortune granddaddy? I want me a fortune!" Little George exclaimed.

Pa-Ty laughed softly and said, "Ain't nothing to it boy. Just two or three things you gotta do Lil' Bully." Pa- Ty grunted as he moved his body around on the hay to ease the pain from the giant hernia.

"How, how granddaddy, how can I make my fortune?" Little George was really excited now. "Having more money than can be counted?' Wow!" he thought. Pa-Ty motioned with his index finger for Little George to come closer. Pa-Ty's voice was becoming faint. The pain from his hernia made it difficult to breath. Little George placed his ear close to Pa- Ty's dry leathery lips.

Pa-Ty whispered, "When yo money can get full, use some of your dimes to buy the land your shack setting on. Do that as soon as you can boy. Soon as you able, don't never close your eyes at night to rest inside a house that's sitting on another man land, never. You got that boy?" Pa- Ty barked.

"You never make your fortune that way. You got that lii' bully?"

"Yes, sir granddaddy I ain't never gonna shut my eyes to sleep on no other man's land but mine granddaddy."

"Alright, hush up now. Two more things to tell ya. It's
gittin' late." Pa-Ty whispered again in Little George's ear. "When your next can get full, buy the land on each side of yours, then in back of you, and in the front, all the way to the road out yonder. Don't never stop 'lii you own every acre of land between here and heaven." Little George and Pa-Ty laughed and bounced.

"You so funny granddaddy," Little George said. "Why buy the land granddaddy?" Little George was really curious about the idea of buying land.

Pa-Ty said, "Don't seem like the good Lawd interested in making no more of it. Anything the good Lawd done stop making someday be more valuable than gold boy. Do as I say boy. Just do it."

"Okay, granddaddy," Little George said, "OK."

Pa-Ty rested for a few minutes. He was in terrible pain. After a few minutes of silence, Pa-Ty pulled Little George even closer to him. He whispered faintly, "Always own your own mule." Little George laughed again and reminded Pa-Ty that he had already told him to always own his own mule. "Why granddaddy?" Little George asked, "what am I going to do with all that land?"

"First thang you gotta do is own it, rest a come to ya. Ain't got time to go into all that now. Just take what I'm saying on faith and do as I say. You got faith don't ya boy?" Granddaddy asked softly.

"Yes sir, I got faith granddaddy. Cause ...a man who owns the land is a big shot." They laughed again. Pa-Ty became quiet for several minutes. Little George got scared a little. Pa-Ty's eyes shut, but Little George could see that his granddaddy was breathing just fine. After a few minutes Little George softly patted Pa-Ty's shoulder. "Granddaddy, granddaddy, you Okay granddaddy?"

Pa-Ty said, "Yep jest fine. Jest waiting for this pain to turn me a loose. It will pass in a minute." Little George released the air he had been holding in his lungs. "You are strong granddaddy."

Pa-Ty laughed and said, "If this is strong, I hate to see what weak is." They both laughed even harder this time. Another few minutes passed with only silence and Pa-Ty's breathing. Finally, Pa-Ty said, "Lil' Bully, I'm almost afraid to tell ya what I'm about to tell you about building your fortune."

"What are you scared of granddaddy? You ain't ever been scared of anything granddaddy." Little George was shocked. "I gotta admit, I'm as scared of this thing as I'm of disturbing a resting rattle snake."

"What could it be granddaddy? What could it be?" Little George was anxious to know.

Pa-Ty paused for a few long seconds. Finally, he spoke faintly in Little George's ear. "The final secret."

"The final secret granddaddy?" Little George asked loudly.

"Yep," Pa-Ty whispered back.

"Why are you afraid of the final secret granddaddy?"

"It is dangerous in the wrong hands Lil' Bully. The final secret is just like fire, maybe more dangerous. Dangerous beyond your imagination. In right hands, fire is the best friend a fella got. In the wrong hands though, fire brings death and destruction. I must admit I am a little 'fraid boy. Almost rather see ya be a poor dirt floor sharecropper all ya days than for you to get a hold of this powerful secret before you are ready.

The power this final secret can bring ya will destroy ya fer show if ya ain't ready for it. I want have no peace, even in the bosom of the good Lawd if I look down here and see you strutting round here like a wealthy fool, destroying everybody ya come across. No body stand to be around you. Naw, I rather see ya po' all ya days."

What Pa-Ty was saying was making Little George feel sad. "You don't trust me granddaddy? Little George asked, almost tearfully. Pa-Ty said softly, "I trust ya Lil' Bully. Love ya more than I trust ya though. Always remember Lil' Bully, love is more powerful than trust. I just can't do nothing that might hurt yat more than help you." Little George was really disappointed. "You can trust me granddaddy, I promise."

"It ain't just that I'm worried about boy," Pa-Ty explained, "you got more sense in that head of yours than most of the grown fellas running around this here plantation. Most of them act like plum fools. Most of them ain't nothing but boys with whiskers. Ain't worth the salt in their bread. They will always need a fella like you to give them a ride to de field and to church. Help 'em all you kin. They got it honest. Ain't never gonna be no different."

Little George asked, "Then why you don't trust me with the final secret granddaddy?"

Pa-Ty repositioned himself again on the bales of hay to ease the pain that was trying to return. After becoming a bit more comfortable Pa-Ty spoke to Little George rather coarsely, "Didn't say I didn't trust you in de first place. Say I was fraid of the power of the last secret. Whut it do to men ain't ready fer it. I seed fellas started out good as gold. God please wit' 'em. When de money can git full and dey learned de secret, change 'em fore night fall. Wasn't long, nobody could stand be round 'em much. Treated other folks so badly even God turned away from 'em. Lived in hell fore dey died. Don't wont dat fer you Lil' Bully. Rather see you po' all ya days."

"I ain't gon mis treat nobody granddaddy," Little George said. "I'm gonna just take care of you and Grandmamma, and mama, and daddy."

"Whutta bout ya sisters, Cynti and Ceya? Ya daddy, one dem fellas like to dress up like dem ah peacocks. Ain't much for working. Jest like to dress up, strut up'n down the sidewalk. Good fella though. Jest ain't much fer working."

"Um gonna take care all my sisters and brothers, granddaddy, I promise you I will."

"Well, ni, that brother of yourn, Tyrone, ya ain't never go have ta do much fer him. He's a hard worker already. He'll fight too. Ain't gotta worry 'bout him much. You still 'sponsible fo him though."

"Okay granddaddy." Little George said.

"Ni um a little worried 'bout dat baby boy, ol' Butchie boy. He some kinda rascal," Pa-Ty said with a huge smile. "Y'all done already spoil him too much. Gonna be a peacock jest like

ya daddy, ain't never go be much fer working. Jest wanna dress like a peacock and strut around all day. You gonna have ta always make show he git a ride to church."
"I will make sure he get to church granddaddy. Now are you going to tell me the final secret to making a fortune granddaddy, so I can have more money than anybody can count?"

"Aint nothing to that once you learn the secret Lil' Bully. I've seen some of the laziest scoundrels on the good Lawd's earth get richer than a red velvet cake by using the secret. Ain't much to it," Pa-Ty mumbled. "Life pretty simple, when ya know the secret."
"Granddaddy, why everybody don't have a fortune if it so easy granddaddy?"

Pa-Ty said softly, "Jest like I tell before. Thangs easy to do, just as easy not to do. Ain't never gonna be no different. The po' gon always be wit' ya. Ain't never been no different."

"Please granddaddy, please, please, please." Little George begged for the final secret.

Pa-Ty said, "Alright Lil' Bully, I guess I gotta trust ya with it. You gonna drive me plum crazy if'n I don't. Show is afraid though."

"Don't be afraid granddaddy," little George cried. "When I get my fortune, I'm gonna help everybody, granddaddy."

"That's the biggest part of the secret," Pa-Ty said.

"What's that, granddaddy? What is the biggest part of the secret?" Pa-Ty said, "Always think mo' bout serving others than serving yoself. If ya help as many fellas as ya can get what they need, they will make dam sure you end up with a fortune bigger than any man can count. Don't matter what schoolhouse he sat in. Ya got that boy, you got it?"

"Yes, sir, granddaddy I got it."

"Now the second part of the secret is the easy part. Also, the most dangerous. A fella end up ruling the whole world ifn he ain't careful. Cause him to destroy it as well, if he ain't ready for it."

Pa-Ty paused for a moment to catch his breath. "What is it granddaddy? What is the final secret?" Little George's anxiousness was beginning to irritate Pa- Ty a little. Pa-Ty beckoned for Little George to come even closer, as the pain from the hernia was becoming more unbearable, making it very difficult to speak loudly or even breathe.

Little George actually placed his hear close enough to Pa-Ty's lips that he felt his breath. Pa-Ty whispered, "Become the money lender."

"Say what granddaddy?" Little George asked.

"Become the money lender," Pa-Ty repeated softly.

"How do I become the money lender granddaddy?" Little George asked.

Pa-Ty said quietly, "Most fellas run outta money before the month run out. Most of them don't have what they need to feed their families. They have to go to the money lender, and make a loan to get by until the next harvest. They'll starve to death ifn the money lender don't make 'em a loan to get by.

Richest fella on God green Earth always gonna be the money lender. The fella borrowing money, always gonna be the slave to the money lender. Ain't never been no different. Ain't never gonna be no different. Never you be the borrower boy." Pa- Ty barked, gasping for air through the pain. "Ifn you do, you will be a dirt floor sharecropper all ya days. You must always be the money lender. You got that boy?" Pa-Ty said firmly, again and again.

Little George nodded his head. "Yes, sir, granddaddy, I got it…Granddaddy?"

"Yeah boy?"

"How do I become the money lender and how do the money lender get the biggest fortune by giving money away to people?" Little George asked.

Pa-Ty laughed. "The money lender don't give away one brown cent boy. The money lender make a fella a loan and then charge him interest for it. But first, you gotta git your own can filled with dimes. When the fella crossed the road run outta dimes before his wife and chullin fed, he come to you with both his hands stretched out. You put a dime in his hand 'ti! his next harvest."

"Granddaddy?," Little George asked, "What is interest?"

Pa-Ty paused for about six seconds, and then said, "After his harvest come in, the fella bring back the dime he borrowed from, he add a penny to it. That penny is interest. The interest is the amount of money the lender charge the borrower for the loan he made to him. Before long the word get out through these here plantations that there is a money lender close by. Every fella in Edgefield County, colored and white, will beat a path to your door step one time or another.

"Every fella be down on his luck every now and then. Can't feed his wife and chullin. Come to you for help. A man worth the salt in his bread can't stand to see his wife and his chullin hungry. He'll pay most anything for the loan. I seen some fellas pay as much as five pennies on every dime loan to him and don't complain a bit. Yea Lil' Bully, if you practice this final secret, you will unleash a power greater than thunder and lighting. You will be king of the entire world in no time flat."

 "King of the whole world granddaddy?" Little George exclaimed, as he strutted around with his chest stuck out so far, his rib cage was showing.

"Yep!" said Pa-Ty, "you will be able to dress like a peacock every day of your life ifn you wanna. Your wife and chullin dress like peacocks too. You be able to practice the golden rule."

Little George said with excitement, "Granddaddy, you already taught me the golden rule!"

"What is it then boy?" Pa-Ty's deep voice rumbled with pride.

Little George proudly said, "Do unto others as you want them to do unto you."

Pa-Ty laughed and clapped his hands and said, "You got it boy. Don't ever forget that one. But there is another golden rule almost as important as the first one."

"What rule is that granddaddy?" Little George could hardly contain his emotions.

Pa-Ty smiled and said, "The fella that got the gold make the rule." Pa-Ty and Little George laughed and laughed. Pa-Ty suddenly became serious. He said, "but remember Iii' Bully, why the peacock dress up and strut around all day." Little George stopped strutting around, pretending to be a peacock, and asked, "Granddaddy, why does the peacock dress up and strut around all day long?"

Pa-Ty pulled Little George close, laughed softly and whispered, "Cause he can't fly. Just like to impress folk I reckon. Nuttin wrong with that ifn that what you wanna do," Pa-Ty said.

"Wealthy man do whatever he want. Ain't never been no different. Ain't never gonna be no different." Little George became quiet he did not like the sound of what he had just heard from Pa-Ty.

After a moment of silence, Little George yelled, "Granddaddy, I ain't gonna be like no peacock. I ain't gonna try to impress nobody. When I build my fortune granddaddy, I'm gonna take care of you and Grandmamma and all my sisters and brothers. I'm gonna build you a whole hospital granddaddy, so you can be operated on."

Pa-Ty laughed very hard until the pain from his hernia made him stop. Little George continued to promise. He said, "Even when I get my fortune, I'm gonna keep on helping as many people as I can make their ends meet and feed their wives and children. I'm gonna buy all the land on God's green Earth granddaddy, just like you say."

Pa-Ty laughed very hard again and spoke softly. "You got it Lil' Bully. You really got it. Just remember, the same thang it take to build a fortune, the same thang it take to keep one. Ain't never been no different. Little George softly answered, "Yes, Granddaddy?"

"Remember, a fortune can be lost a lot quicker than it take to be built, especially ifn you spend too much time strutting like a peacock." Little George hugged Pa-Ty as hard as he could. And they just hugged and laughed.
Pa-Ty suddenly barked, "Get outta here Lil' Bully, ya can't build no fortune hanging up in here with me and ol' Dalla. Get outta here now. I wanna talk with ol' Dalla here for while…"

Most of the night, Little George laid on his hay filled mattress on his back looking at the streaks of moon light that were squeezing through the cracks in the tin roof. He was dreaming about his life as the richest man in the world.

He could see his beautiful mansion surrounded by acres of giant pine trees. There was so much land, the boundary could not be seen from the front porch or the back porch. He had visions of ten-inch-long catfish flying up out of his private pond. Perfect vegetables, turnips, collards, kale, and corn. Golden peaches as far as the eye could see. Corn as tall as most men.

He envisioned children and his grandchildren running through the lush fields surrounding his mansion as they play tag. He could see thousands of people lined up in front of his door seeking a dollar to help make their ends meet until harvest time as he watched from his high porch.

He dreamt of taking hams and sweet potatoes thorough the back woods to offer poor families like he witnessed standing around the fire barrels, just like Pa-Ty used to do. "I just can't wait to be rich," he kept repeating to himself. "I can't wait to be rich. I'm gonna be the money lender," he said to himself, over and over and over.

Suddenly, he was asleep. Sunshine bursting through the cracks in the roof awakened him from his wonderful dreams. He only got a couple of hours of sleep the entire night. Little George was curious why Pa-Ty had not come to his bed and barked at him for sleeping too late. He loved Pa-Ty's rough deep voice.

He rubbed the sleep from his eyes with his two-little fist. He slowly rolled off his hay stuffed mattress. Little George was attacked by the early morning cold. It was eerily, cold and quiet throughout the entire shack

There was no fire in the fire place, nor in the black potbellied stove in Grandmamma Nannie's kitchen. There were no grits, gravy, biscuits, or the odor of bacon attacking his nostrils, as had occurred every other morning as far back as he could remember. Little George hastily got dressed. He put on his heavy wool coat and Brogan boots. It was really too cold in the house.

Little George peeked his head out of his bedroom door. "Grandmamma...Grandmamma!" he yelled out. There was only silence, and the cold. He slowly checked each room in the house.

"Granddaddy, Uncle Buddy!" he called out. There was only silence. Little George finally arrived shivering at the front door, which was cracked open. "No wonder it's so cold in here," he thought. Little George walked out on to the porch.

He noticed a strange looking dingy white mule hooked to a long, wooden buggy in front of the shed where Pa-Ty's beloved mule Dalla was kept. Little George became a little scared. He hoped Dalla was okay. He remembered that he had left Pa-Ty in the shed last night talking with Dalla.

There was a very skinny little man sitting in the driver's seat of the wagon. Little George was curious why the creepy little man was wearing a black suit and hat on a Saturday. The man was dressed like the preacher man from old Macedonia Baptist church, except for the tall black hat and white gloves.

Little George began to get scared again, especially when he saw the entire family standing around the wagon. Grandmamma Nannie's face was buried in the palm of her hands. Little George thought again, "Hope Dalla alright." But he had his doubts. He knew if something happened to Dalla his Granddaddy could hardly take it. He was just so scared.

Little George jumped off of the porch and began walking toward the shed. "Poor Dalla," he thought. Suddenly, Dalla poked her head out of the shed door and bobbled it up and down. She made her normal gruffy sounds. Little George exhaled. "Thank you, dear God," he thought to himself again. Little George walked closer and closer to the horse drawn wagon. The preacher looking man wearing the tall black hat and white gloves waved his right hand. Little George was not certain, but he thought he heard the skinny man whisper the words, "My sympathies."

Little George was terrified now. He did not see his granddaddy Pa-Ty. That's when he saw it. He noticed the elongated wooden box lying flat in the back of the wagon. The box was covered with a white sheet.

Before Little George walked closer Uncle Buddy and Uncle Bosie began to yell at him. "Go back inside Little George! Get back into the house!" They were yelling very loudly. Little George ignored them.

Uncle Buddy and Uncle Bosie angrily yelled again, "Go back in the house boy!" Little George again ignored them. He just kept walking toward the shed. Uncle Buddy and Bosie started running towards him. Little George suddenly felt a sense of horrible dread.

Bosie and Buddy grabbed him and lifted him up off the ground. Little George began to kick and fight his uncles. He screamed "Granddaddy! Granddaddy! I'm gonna tell granddaddy on y'all." Bosie and Buddy were too strong. They carried Little George back to the porch. They held him down on the wooden porch until the skinny man dressed in black rode slowly out his sight.

Little George knew without any doubt. He knew that it was his granddaddy, the old industrious Edgefield County sharecropper lying in that wooden box. He knew that his granddaddy was about to be thrown down the slave hole.

Sadness ravaged Little George's entire body and soul. He found some comfort in knowing that finally, Pa-Ty was going to be with his beloved pappy and mammy again. Little George knew in his heart, that's what Pa-Ty longed for. He also knew the watermelon sized hernia hanging from Pa- Ty's private parts finally squeezed the life out of his granddaddy. Little George pondered and pondered why didn't they take him to the hospital?" Little George never got an answer. Deep down in his soul, he knew the answer. He could hear Pa-Ty McKie's wisdom, "Rich man do as he please."

A few days after the funeral Little George left the Burke plantation. Never to return, except to bring his children and grandchildren to visit the place where their great grandfather, the industrious 50% sharecropper, the Rev. Pa-Ty McKie lived, labored, fed his family and died. The McKie family was given two weeks to vacate the land and make room for the next sharecropper family.

Little George always remembered every nugget of financial wisdom Pa-Ty taught him. He knew the exact formula for becoming rich and wealthy, and how to make a fortune so grand, that nobody could count his money.

Little George promised his granddaddy, as he stood over the slave hole, behind the old Macedonia Baptist church, just off of highway 25 in Edgefield County, South Carolina, that he would never become a "peacock." That he would become a man of wealth, richness, faith, and dignity. Pa-Ty McKie's bones mixed with his beloved mammy and pappy lie unmarked behind that old church that he loved so dearly, to this very day.

Little George promised his granddaddy that he would never close his eyes at night on land owned by another "fella." That he would always seek to give more than he got. Always give the preacher his dime. Always put three dimes out of every dollar that came to him through labor or gift, in the money can.

He promised to buy all the land he could manage. The final secret he kept sacred to his heart. Be the money lender, never the borrower. Little George, with tears flooding down his cheeks, promised his granddaddy, that for the rest of his life he would use the "Secret" to honor his legacy by building a financial fire wall around himself and our family that nothing could penetrate. He promised, again, to never become a peacock for as long as he lived.

Little George, the grandson of the legendary Black sharecropper Pa-Ty McKie, currently resides in Augusta, Georgia. He enjoys fifty years of marriage to his beloved and devoted wife. His beloved was born in a small southern town in south Georgia.

They entered into permanent matrimony when she was just 17 years of age years old and had just graduated from High School. Little George was 21. Like the lyrics to one of Nat King Coles' greatest hits, "They tried to tell Us We're too Young", too young to really be in love."

His chosen beloved's elders relented to the union only after weeks of them begging, crying, and promising that their daughter would complete her college education uninterrupted. The love birds made and kept their promise to the elders. Little George's beloved completed her bachelor's degree and master's degree with the highest honors and in record speed.

Little George never engaged in any formal educational process post high school. He proudly shares that he never earned more than nine dollars an hour of wages during his entire life. He always remembered that his granddaddy taught him that wages were less important than profits, and that it is not how much you make that matters, but how much you invest that creates your fortune.

Little George never forgot a single one of Pa-Ty McKie's financial wisdom. He activated each of these simple wisdoms into every aspect of his life with amazing results. He also passed down Pa-Ty's financial wisdoms to his sons. Both of these talented young men are college graduates and have left the comforts of their parents' wealth, to begin creating their own individual fortunes for themselves and their families.

Empty nesters now, Little George, and his beloved reside on a private gated, twenty plus -acre debt- free estate. The estate is eerily similar to the Burke plantation in Edgefield, South Carolina, including a replica of the catfish pond where Pa-Ty bestowed upon Little George the wisdoms to riches. Little George's beloved recently returned from a month- long luxury cruise though Europe.

The End.